Sensual Love Secrets
FOR COUPLES

Sensual Love Secrets

FOR COUPLES

THE FOUR FREEDOMS OF
BODY, MIND, HEART & SOUL

AL LINK & PALA COPELAND

Llewellyn Publications
Woodbury, Minnesota

First Edition
First Printing, 2007

Back cover photograph by Bill Ling / © Digital Vision
Book design and layout by Joanna Willis
Cover design by Gavin Dayton Duffy
Cover photograph © Barnaby Hall/Photonica/Getty Images

Llewellyn is a registered trademark of Llewellyn Worldwide, Ltd.

Library of Congress Cataloging-in-Publication Data
The Cataloging-in-Publication Data for *Sensual Love Secrets for Couples* is on file at the Library of Congress.
ISBN-13: 978-0-7387-0965-9
ISBN-10: 0-7387-0965-4

Llewellyn Publications
A Division of Llewellyn Worldwide, Ltd.
2143 Wooddale Drive, Dept. 0-7387-0965-4
Woodbury, MN 55125-2989, U.S.A.
www.llewellyn.com

Printed in the United States of America

CONTENTS

EXERCISES

INTRODUCTION

Right this moment, just as you are, you have four unimaginably powerful resources at your command. With them you can accomplish miracles. They are your Four Freedoms of Body, Mind, Heart, and Soul. Although you are innately aware of these elemental forces—their strength, dynamism, and wonder—the wise inner voice of your higher self becomes overwhelmed in a world of speed, superficiality, and complexity. Reclaiming your Four Freedoms helps you to hear truth again, to remember who you are and why you are in a body, and to gain emotional stability and courage as well as mental clarity and focused attention. The Four Freedoms framework gives you a secure platform when your world begins to tremble and quake.

The essence of freedom is choice. Embracing your Four Freedoms helps you become aware of the choices available to you and gives you the strength to act on them. If you fear that by diving headlong into freedom you will act selfishly or irresponsibly—considering only your ego's wants—remember that such thoughts are part of the captive mentality that claims that the nature of humanity is evil and therefore must be denied or contained. The truth is that you are intrinsically glorious and worthy, despite your flaws. You always have the choice of acting from your shortcomings or acting from your greatness. When you are really free, you will naturally act for the greatest good of yourself and others, because that is the true nature of your highest self.

As you begin to explore your Four Freedoms, you might feel more comfortable with one or two and want to gloss over or ignore the others. If you are intensely emotional, you might resist exercising your rationality. An overriding mental focus might block you from enjoying the pleasures of your body. A potent physicality might distract you from the realm of spirit. Or, preferring to seek peace in the inner realm of soul, you might shy away from the turbulence of emotion and the temptations of pleasure. However, you will not have the relationship you long for by suppressing or denying any of your Four Freedoms. You must embrace, explore, and balance all—Body, Mind, Heart, and Soul—no matter how irrelevant or frightening the components might seem.

Freedom is not just an intellectual or philosophical idea. You manifest freedom in your behavior. You choose and you act. Use the platform of the Four Freedoms to help you make your choices. They will let you know when there is something new to learn or something old to unlearn. Unfortunately, you cannot change merely by thinking about it. To both learn and unlearn effectively, you need to adjust your behavior. Behavioral changes help shift your thoughts and feelings about yourself by providing positive feedback when you act in new ways. Behavioral changes are more effective than simply trying to alter thought patterns loaded with years of conditioned beliefs and assumptions. Some changes you'll make on your own; others you'll tackle together with your partner.

The good news is that you don't have to wait until you're certain you can create an exceptional relationship before you enter into one. You really become fit for a relationship only by being in a relationship. You learn by doing, because your relationship is most definitely an experiential phenomenon. The ongoing practice of integrating your Four Freedoms enhances your relationship. In turn, your strengthened relationship amplifies your personal growth and quickens your spiritual progress. Your relationship and your spiritual journey are mutually supportive. Indeed, your relationship can become your spiritual practice.

As you continue along your path of freedom, you will also receive support from the universe, because creating love over a lifetime is a developmental process that synchronizes with the natural order by aligning the forces of change, learning, and loving. You begin to understand that you will not become whole or free by finding your missing half in a loving partner. Rather, two whole people recognize each other as soul mates and learn the skills needed to create love for a joyous lifetime together. The Four Freedoms—Body Freedom, Mind Freedom, Heart Freedom, and Soul Freedom—are the building blocks for the relationship you crave so deeply.

part 1
THE FOUR FREEDOMS

THE DESIRE TO LOVE SOMEONE through and through and to be loved that way in return, for a lifetime, burns in almost every heart. Although we are all truly worthy of such love, it is not something that will usually happen by itself. A superb relationship, one that satisfies and stimulates to the core, is an extraordinary accomplishment, comparable to supreme achievement in realms of business, the arts, science, and sports. Such relationships are rare not because people lack the capacity for loving but because they don't know how to make the shift from falling in love to sustaining that love over many years by creating and recreating it again and again.

You might believe that continuously creating love is an impossibly daunting task. Perhaps you've been through painful unions before, and your heart is battered and broken. Or your present relationship, although comfortable, has become just a little boring, stuck in a rut of mundane sameness. Then again, you might be at the outset of a wondrous romance and only slightly haunted by a nagging suspicion that your passion will eventually fade. Whatever your present circumstances, do not allow preconceptions and fears to impede your heart's aspirations. Living a lifelong, passionate, and intimate union is not a complicated undertaking. On the contrary, it is quite simple and well within your abilities. The fundamental requirement? Rediscover and reunite your Four Freedoms: Body, Mind, Heart, and Soul. These Four Freedoms are the essence of human nature—yours and everyone else's.

The First Freedom: BODY

Awaken your senses. See, hear, smell, taste, and feel love. Know your body as a divine temple of love, carrier of your soul, manifestation of God and Goddess. Become truly at home in your body, at ease and at peace in your skin. Allow yourself to experience physical pleasure. Feed yourself and all those around you with sublime, intimate, human touch. You are your body. Your body is freedom.

The Second Freedom: MIND

There are no limits. All limits are self-imposed. Change thought from your master to your powerful servant, a tool of your liberation. Turn your thinking on, and turn it off, when *you* want to. You have power over what you think about. You also have power over *how* you think about what you think about. Connect with your higher self for guidance and direction. You are your mind. Your mind is freedom.

The Third Freedom: HEART

Heal your broken heart. Open your healed heart. Give and receive love easily, naturally, spontaneously, and unconditionally. Discover your lover within. Love yourself. Accept yourself. Forgive yourself. Know that you are worthy of love. Acknowledge and welcome the love of others. Dare to be the great lover you are. You are your heart. Your heart is freedom.

The Fourth Freedom: SOUL

Your body, mind, and heart are windows to your soul. Soul transcends space and time. It is outside of cause and effect. Soul is complete and perfect. When you communicate with your higher self, with God and Goddess, you are communicating with Soul. Soul has your body, mind, and heart within it. Soul is what you are. Your soul is part of the Soul. Your soul is freedom.

$\mathcal{T}$HE FIRST FREEDOM:
body

You do not have to be good.
    You do not have to walk on your knees for a hundred miles through the desert, repenting.
    You only have to let the soft animal of your body love what it loves.

Mary Oliver,
"Wild Geese"[1]

The Goddess is first of all earth, the dark, nurturing mother who brings forth all life. She is the power of fertility and generation; the womb, and also the receptive tomb, the power of death. All proceeds from Her; all returns to Her. As earth, She is also plant life; trees, the herbs and grains that sustain life.
    She is the body, and the body is sacred.

Starhawk,
The Spiral Dance[2]

Body Marvels

Your body is an extraordinary organism: an electrical, chemical, and mechanical marvel. Its trillions of individual cells array themselves in complex combinations to produce the physical wonder that is at once uniquely you and at the same time like every other human being. Bodies have more exciting bits and carry out more strenuous tasks than you've probably ever imagined. For instance, although you've not likely counted them, five million hairs sprout from the 36 to 60 square feet (3.3 to 5.6 square meters) of durable, waterproof covering you know as skin. Beneath this living overcoat are three types of muscles, your "movers and shakers," more than 600 in all, which connect to, and are supported by, the 206 bones forming your skeleton. This lightweight framework is not only flexible, but also incredibly strong. Your thigh bones, for example, are pound for pound stronger than reinforced concrete.

Throughout your body, intricate delivery systems transport nutrients and information for survival and action. Every day your heart beats 100,000 times, pumping 300 quarts (284 liters) of blood per hour through 90,000 miles (145,000 kilometers) of blood vessels, keeping you warm, nourishing your cells, removing waste, and destroying harmful substances. Your internal communication network, the nervous system, controls and coordinates most of your body's activities with electrical impulses that travel at speeds of up to 250 miles per hour (400 kilometers per hour). Much slower and longer lasting are the chemical reactions governed by your hormonal system that affect when and how you grow, the density of your bones, the intensity of your sex drive, and the onset of puberty, menopause, and andropause.

Not only does your body keep you functioning fairly smoothly throughout your allotted lifespan, but it also carries within it the keys to ensure survival of future generations. At birth, a woman's ovaries already cradle up to two million eggs, any of which can mature to mate with one of the more than several hundred million sperm a typical man produces daily. The result of this passionate joining is a zygote that, although smaller than the head of a pin, contains every bit of the genetic information needed to create a new, one-of-a-kind human being.

All of this boisterous activity requires energy derived from oxygen and food. In a lifetime, the average person will breathe about 75 million gallons (285 million liters) of air and consume up to 50 tons (45 metric tons) of food. Built-in taste and aroma sensors entice you to feed your body. Nine thousand taste buds adorn your tongue, beguiling you with five distinct flavors and their thousands of combined permutations. The ten million olfactory receptacles in your nose can distinguish 10,000 separate scents.

Your body is a sensory cornucopia. In addition to taste and smell, sight, sound, and touch contribute to the wealth of sensate experience available to you. Your eyes can identify ten million different colors. Your ears can hear more than 400,000 unique sounds. Your skin has thousands of miniscule, highly sensitive receptors that make it a head-to-toe communication source more eloquent than words.[3]

Sensual Nutrition

Your body is a remarkable gift from the Creator, a vehicle through which the spiritual can experience the material. That is what a body is for. As spirit in physical form, you can celebrate and explore the sensory joys of this gift. Come to your senses—all of them. Absorb right here, right now, what you see, hear, smell, taste, and touch. Direct sensory stimulation is nourishment for your body—sensual nutrition, another kind of food without which it cannot thrive and be free. The freedom of the senses is the freedom to experience pleasure and feel desire, to know you are truly alive.

Body Freedom enables you to behold and be warmed by the brightest light of all: the consuming light of love shining from your sweetheart's eyes. It allows you to revel in the husky whispers and throaty moans that are music to a lover's ears. To freely devour succulent kisses from pouty lips tasting of fruit and honey. To sniff hungrily and absorb the distinctive scent that is uniquely your beloved's. To touch and touch and touch with fingers, palms, lips, and tongues, then to lie at ease in each other's arms, safe, secure, sympathetic, blessed . . .

Sadly, you might not perceive your body as a biological marvel, a sensory gateway, the temple of your soul. Like many, you might have forgotten your Body Freedom, been indoctrinated to view your body as ugly and sinful, a prison[4] that will never be beautiful enough or strong enough, will never measure up no matter what you do, that constantly betrays you with its shameful desires and ultimately keeps you separate and lonely.

All bodies are naturally beautiful, because they are the earthly home of your eternal soul, but this is not likely the message you most often hear. Your body perception is under attack on multiple fronts. For instance, many religious teachings perpetuate negative body images, either decrying the body as unclean and shameful or dismissing it as a distraction from higher purposes. If you want spiritual purity, you are exhorted to ignore your body's wants and wishes.

From a commercial perspective, no body is ever quite beautiful enough. You are bulldozed into seeing your physical self as an ongoing renovation project. From skin tone to hair color, from breast and penis size to length of leg and girth of waist, from laughlines to crow's feet, there's always room for improvement. Under continued social pressure, you might come to see your body through tainted eyes, developing an emotionally and physically damaging dissatisfaction with your natural form. You might give yourself and others sabotaging messages that continue to erode your Body Freedom.

Desire for the "perfect" body might lead you into life-threatening eating disorders, as it has about seven million women and one million men in the United States.[5] Or it might entice you into the cosmetic surgeon's office for procedures ranging from Botox injections to chemical peels, from liposuction to breast augmentation, from hair transplants to facelifts. Cosmetic procedures are multiplying by leaps and bounds. In 2005 alone, American cosmetic surgeons performed more than 11.5 million procedures, up a whopping 444 percent from 1997.[6] Perhaps you might even be tempted to join the ranks of thousands in both the United States and Britain who apply to be a contestant on reality shows such as *Extreme Makeover*. These very popular television series feature the ultimate in body redesign, employing teams of specialists—plastic surgeons, eye surgeons, cosmetic dentists, hair and makeup artists, stylists, and personal trainers—to radically alter a participant's appearance. The premise, as outlined on ABC's website, is to give participants "a truly Cinderella-like experience by changing your looks completely in an effort to transform your life and destiny, and to make your dreams come true."[7]

People try to make their bodies beautiful so that others will love them, admire them, reward them, and accept them. It would be better to learn simply to love your body and so to become free and lovable in it. However, it's often easier to blame your equipment and try to make it conform to someone else's ideal than to learn about it, listen to it, and honor it for yourself.

Body Pleasure and Relationship

Fortunately, a mate relationship gives you a perfect arena in which to learn to overcome your negative body conditioning and to celebrate your body's desires. When you are in a loving relationship, consciously sharing your body with another, you can become more at ease in your skin. Under the adoring gaze and lusty caresses of your mate, you can learn to know your beauty from the inside out. A fulfilling sex life assists you in feeling beautiful through channels that are both chemical (mood-altering endorphins) and emotional (the intimacy of desire). If you feel beautiful, you are.

As integral aspects of deep connection between lovers, pleasure, touching, and sex gain moral legitimacy and spiritual character in the context of a monogamous relationship. Monogamous relationships provide a cocoon of commitment, a safe haven for learning the ways of Body Freedom. Consider, for example, touch as one of the most basic sources of pleasure. Touch isn't optional for a good relationship, it's essential. Studies dating back more than fifty years document that without touch, human beings do not thrive.[8] Without touch, you can become emotionally withdrawn and physically and psychically ill. The absence of pleasure might induce emotional instability, possibly correlated with addiction, and encourage abusive, violent behavior.[9] Relationships give you permission to explore touching in intimate ways that range from tenderly affectionate to passionately sexual. Physical pleasure becomes socially acceptable within the context of a relationship.

Affectionate touch and satisfying sex nourish you and your relationship. Sensual nutrition is not just in your head, and it's definitely more than skin-deep. As Lou Reed sings, "I think it's chemical." When you give and receive loving, sensual touch, endorphins and oxytocin surge through your system. Not only do these powerful chemicals make you feel great while you're caressing, but they also fuel the desire for more touches later. By upping your touch quotient, you can satisfy more than just your partner's skin hunger; stress release, comfort, relaxation, and healing are all at your fingertips.

Contrary to the stereotypes that men primarily want sexual touching and women mostly want affectionate touching, both forms are equally important for enduring, satisfying relationships. Men and women alike crave nonsexual touching. Owing as much to cultural conditioning as to physiological makeup, men are usually more accustomed to intimate touching that is sexual. But once they experience it, men love to be touched in nonsexual ways as well. Such caresses help break through times of low self-esteem, fear, and doubt. With a tender hug or gentle pat, you can give comfort and acceptance and create a strong, loving bond that goes beyond the physical. When touching is only sexual, however, you might feel that you are being solicited to perform sexually or that you are valued primarily as a sexual object.

Touch is essential for a good relationship.

If you already touch each other frequently, keep doing it. If you don't, begin now—today. You can start simply by bestowing an encouraging squeeze of the shoulder as your partner attends to a household chore, by exchanging a hug as you leave for work, or by sitting side-by-side holding hands and snuggling toes as you watch TV.

Casual, unfocused caresses while you're essentially engaged in some other activity, like watching a movie, can be delightful, but for the most part remember to put conscious attention into your touch. Be completely present. Bring your mind, heart, and soul in. Do not allow yourself to fall into absent-minded habitual strokes that carry no meaning. Are you all there when you embrace your partner? Or is part of you at the office, grocery store, hockey game, or committee meeting? Become fully aware of the messages you give with your rubs, pats, and hugs.

Put conscious attention into your touch.

Mate relationships include sexual caresses as well as compassionate and comradely ones. If you don't have sex, then it's a different kind of union—platonic—more akin to friendship than marriage. Mate relationships make sex permissible and safe both physically and emotionally. In a committed relationship, sex is elevated. It gains moral force because it becomes not only a source of great physical pleasure but also a key expression of love.

Economists David Blanchflower and Andrew Oswald suggest that the happiest people are those getting the most sex, and that sex has a bigger influence on happiness than money. Their conclusions are based on data from a random sample of sixteen thousand adult Americans. They claim that "increasing intercourse from once a month to once a week is equivalent to the amount of happiness generated by getting an additional $50,000 in income . . . and a lasting marriage equates to happiness generated by getting an extra $100,000 each year. Divorce, meanwhile, translates to a happiness depletion of $66,000 annually."[10] Another study by researchers at Georgia State University concludes that involuntarily celibate people "are frequently afflicted with nonhappy feelings—anger, frustration, self-doubt, and even depression."[11]

Although most couples want a really good sex life, many are afraid that it's unattainable because they personally don't know how to create it. They bury their sexual dreams under the weight of misinformation that says, "Sex is something you should just naturally know how to do because you're in a body." However, even though your body desires and has the potential for sublime sex, it doesn't automatically know the artistry of lovemaking. You must teach the body. Like any great art, the art of sexual ecstasy must be learned. Sexual knowledge and skill develop over a lifetime. If you travel through your sexual life in a learning mode, then your sexual experience will continue to improve over the years. It will grow with you as you grow.

Sexual knowledge develops over a lifetime.

Transforming Your Sexuality

As a couple, you can extend the passion and satisfaction of your sexual life by evolving your regular sex into sacred sex. For thousands of years, and in a variety of cultures, sacred sex practices have affirmed the core message that sex is good—namely, an integral part of life connecting you to yourself, to your partner, and to the Divine. Sacred sex shifts the focus of sex from achieving orgasm to union and pleasure. Lovemaking is expanded beyond the common understanding of sex as intercourse to include all manner of intimate contact. Sacred sex is a practical way to balance the purely physiological differences between men and women. Women gain the time their bodies need to be thoroughly aroused and totally satisfied in addition to receiving the affection and emotional connection they want. Men receive lots of explicit sexual activity, but, because intercourse is interspersed with other forms of sensual play, they are able to last long enough for their lovers' gratification. Both partners experience greater pleasure and intimacy.

Experience all your senses, always.

In sacred sex, you honor your body as a temple for your spirit and offer it as a gift to your lover. This approach sanctifies your body, asserting its beauty and magnificence. Shame and guilt disappear as you move beyond repression and give yourself permission to experience all your senses at every moment.

Claiming Your Body Freedom

Divesting yourself of your body's armor, so that you can be fully at ease in your body and share it completely with your beloved, requires learning a few new things and unlearning some old ones. In addition to the common misperceptions already mentioned (people naturally know how to make love, and touch is optional), you'll come up against others. You'll need to replace limiting, sabotaging notions with body-affirming and relationship-building ideas. This transformation includes:

Letting go of "Pleasure, touching, and sex are dangerous, bad, and sinful" and affirming that "Pleasure, touching, and sex are biological, emotional, and spiritual needs—sensual nutrition."

Shifting "My lover is responsible for my pleasure" to "I am responsible for my pleasure." No matter how skilled, adoring, or attentive your partner may be, unless you allow yourself to be open to pleasure, you won't experience it.

Transforming "My partner should know how and when I like to be touched—sexually and nonsexually" into "I have to let my partner know what I like and need." Very few are mind readers when it comes to lovemaking, and sex is one place where you don't follow the golden rule of "Do unto others as you'd have others do unto you." Everyone has individual preferences for loving touch, so push past your barriers of shame, guilt, or embarrassment and ask for what you want.

Changing "Sexual touching is the most intimate touching" into "Nonsexual touching is just as intimate as sexual touching." *Intimate* describes the quality of your touch, not the activity itself. Intimacy goes far beyond the physical. The deepest intimacy is grounded in an emotional, energetic, and spiritual connection that you can cultivate through both sexual and nonsexual touch.

Modifying "Young, hard bodies have the best sex" to "Bodies have better sex as they age." Sexual mastery evolves over a lifetime of learning, because great sex requires knowledge and practice. Our culture says young bodies are the sexiest, but simple physical attractiveness doesn't provide the emotional maturity and self-confidence that are essential elements of extraordinary sex.

Qualifying the notion that "Great sex is primarily a matter of physical technique" into the realization that "Great sex combines physical technique with emotional and energetic connection." While skill is definitely an asset in lovemaking, an open heart and a willingness to surrender to your lover makes the difference between sex as pleasant pastime and sex as ecstatic experience.

The best way to learn—and unlearn—is to take action. Remember that your Body Freedom is your responsibility. It is neither mandatory nor automatic. You can claim your Body Freedom with the following actions:

1. Pay attention to your body. Listen to what it tells you about how it feels and what it wants and needs to function at its best, such as good food, enough rest, adequate exercise, and sensory delight.

2. Identify the body-negative messages you give yourself, that others give you, and that you give to others. Replace them with body-positive communication.

3. Touch your mate with tenderness, respect, and caring every day.

4. Change your sexual focus from performance and orgasm to pleasure and union. Dare to learn how to make your sex an ecstatic art.

Claiming your Body Freedom will bring passion and intimacy to your relationship. It will help you feel more secure, more in tune with the natural rhythm of life, and more appreciative of the world's sensory pleasures. You'll discover with paradoxical delight that while your body makes you a unique and separate individual, it is also the perfect medium for merging utterly with another.

$\mathcal{T}$HE SECOND FREEDOM:
mind

Center of the Cyclone

Your mind, center of the cyclone of consciousness, is a remarkable servant. When set to work with clear purpose and direction, it can guide you through a myriad of concepts and activities, from the mundane (Where shall my date and I eat dinner tonight?) to the lofty (Shall I ask my beloved to share the rest of our lives together?) and from the concrete (How do I program the VCR?) to the abstract (Why are we here?). It truly is mind boggling to reflect on the mental accomplishments of humankind as individuals and in concert, from technological invention to artistic creation, from scientific reasoning to metaphysical contemplation.

Thinking about your own mind, you might well locate it in your head and associate it with the processes of your brain, that intricate organ that deciphers information. Your brain, fueled by electrochemical energy, operates a continuous sending/receiving process. There is no "off" switch. Complex functions, such as perception, information processing, and language, occur in the largest portion of your brain, the left and right cerebral hemispheres. Although your electrical brain is located in your head, your "chemical brain" extends throughout your body via a complex network of molecules called receptors and ligands. Their interaction stores emotions and thoughts in cells throughout your entire organism. Your whole body is actively involved in all learning, including the accumulation, storage, and retrieval of memory, feeling, and thought.[1] You have not only a head-brain, but also a body-brain. Your *mind*, however, is much more than your elaborate biological hardware.

Mind is your consciousness interface between the biological—the brain, the central nervous system, the heart, and the rest of the physical human body—and other sources of awareness, including your subconsciousness, the collective consciousness, and the superconsciousness. Mind assimilates *all* the sources of consciousness that generate the information inputs that the body-brain receives and decodes: "For all that lives and all that ever has is part of a collective brain, a neural net of the most sprawling kind . . . an evolution-driven, worldwide, multi-billion-year-old interspecies mind."[2]

Imagine that consciousness is like water:

- Your personal consciousness is the supply of water you can carry around in a canteen, as if it belonged to you privately, for your exclusive use. With this personal consciousness, you think, perceive, feel, and make choices.

- The collective consciousness is the supply of fresh water the planet provides for the global tribe of humanity. It is a shared consciousness, common to all human beings, although few have learned how to make full use of it. Those who have learned experience what is commonly called ESP (extrasensory perception), some forms of which are telepathy, clairvoyance, astral projection, and remote viewing.

- The superconsciousness (also known as Cosmic Consciousness or God Consciousness) is the infinite supply of water falling to planet Earth from the heavens. Totally impersonal, it is readily available to everyone free of charge. Although only rare individuals regularly access this consciousness, those who do experience mystical perceptions, e.g., *samadhi*, nirvana, or enlightenment.

Because your mind is connected to all these resources and your brain never shuts down, your mind is working for you even when it is off duty. Your dreams can give you guidance. Solutions to complicated problems often arise when you've stopped thinking about the answer and left things to percolate for a while. Sudden flashes of inspiration and insight ("aha!" moments) seem to arrive out of nowhere.

When your mind is in its natural state, pure and clear, it serves you extremely well, but when it becomes tangled in the delusions of daily life, it can switch from helpful servant to disruptive master. Random thoughts of past and future prevent you from enjoying the present. Memory tapes of failure and unworthiness can keep you in a loop of unfulfilled potential. Deeply ingrained prejudices can blind you from seeing for yourself. It's time to reclaim your Mind Freedom.

Mind Freedom

The essence of mind is consciousness. The freedom of mind is attention and intention. The responsibility of mind is choice.

Witness Consciousness: The Power of Self-Awareness

Retraining your mind to become once again your servant rather than your master requires you to develop self-awareness. Whether positive or negative, your mind approaches life in its own particular and unique way. You might be the only person in the whole world who does what you do exactly the way you do it. If you pay careful attention and attempt to be an objective observer, your "witness consciousness" or "observer consciousness" can identify exactly how your mind operates. Being aware of what you do inside your head enables you to name it. Then, "the truth shall set you free," because naming empowers you. When you name what you are doing, you gain emotional distance from it and so can choose to stop or to continue. This is freedom.

Witness Consciousness = Self-Awareness

Because of the speed, complexity, and fragmentation of the world, you cannot pay attention to the vast overload of information. You must choose what you'll focus on. Making choices is the foundation of all Four Freedoms. In Mind Freedom, there are two levels of choice:

1. *What* you think about—your attention

2. *How* you think about what you think about—your intention

An axiom of Mind Freedom is that *you get more of what you pay attention to.* A little-understood corollary is that *attention equals choice.* In other words, *you are choosing to have more of the subject matter of your attention.*

Attention = Choice

Use your witness consciousness to become aware of *what* and *how* you are thinking from moment to moment. You can choose to pay attention to what you want, rather than what you don't want. An enlightened human being pays attention to or thinks about only what he *does* want. This is one meaning of higher consciousness. Although it is impossible to prevent all negative thoughts from entering your mind, you can always choose whether to pay attention to them or to let them go. Furthermore, if you choose to think about something, you can think about it in a positive way. By doing so, you own both your attention and intention, and your mind remains a faithful servant. It taps into all its resources and presents you with opportunities to actually make your ideas happen. Then, of course, you must act to support your thoughts. By taking action, you give your servant (your mind) a reward and a powerful encouragement to continue serving you well.

Keys to Mind Freedom

Witness consciousness—*Self-awareness*

Attention—*What*

Intention—*How*

Employing Mind Freedom to Empower Your Relationship

Conscious Attention to What Matters

The world is demanding and constantly changing. People tend to ignore one of their most important anchors for intellectual sanity, emotional security, and spiritual wisdom—their primary relationship with a mate. A committed, lifelong relationship with another human being is a simple, obvious, and profound source of happiness, but relationships ring in low on many couples' list of priorities. Although people might say their relationship is very important, their actual behavior contradicts them. Individuals become preoccupied with worldly matters (careers, material goods, social position) and begin to take their partners for granted. When attention goes elsewhere, the relationship anchor cuts loose, and the relationship drifts out to sea.

This situation does not just happen to you. You are not the helpless victim of a world characterized by the popular (albeit misinformed) saying "Life is hard and then you die." In fact, you are a co-creator of your situation, and you can just as easily create something different and new using the power of Mind Freedom.

How to Think about Your Relationship

Relationship success flows from paying sustained attention to your relationship. How you think about your relationship is typically dictated by learned beliefs and assumptions, many of which are negative and can lead you from one relationship failure to another. Become aware of relationship-negative messages you give yourself and others, and then intentionally shift them to positive messages.

Here are two examples:

1. **Having time for each other.** Want more time with your partner?
   a. Focus on your desire to be together. Picture the moments you've had together and the pleasure that brings.
   b. If other thoughts begin to whiningly intrude ("But we have so much to do," "We can't take time, even though I want to," "Other things are more pressing"), let them pass through.
   c. Replace them with: "We do have a lot going on in our lives, but we're important and I want more time together. I know we can find some way to make that happen."
   d. Possibilities will present themselves; situations will arise when you can choose to spend time together or not. Seize those opportunities.

2. **Sustaining your relationship.** Want to spend a lifetime with your mate?
   a. Picture the two of you growing happy and healthy together into old age.
   b. When learned assumptions insinuate themselves into your head ("Most relationships don't last," "Passion dies," "Lovers grow apart"), send them out the window.
   c. Replace them with: "Our relationship will thrive throughout the years."
   d. Act on every opportunity that emerges to intensify your connection.

Thought Experiment

At first, use this experiment to focus on your relationship with your partner. Later you can use the same technique for other important aspects of your life.

Endeavor for one day to think only about what you *do* want. Whenever you catch yourself thinking about what you don't want, gently stop and refocus your attention onto what you *do* want, even if you believe it isn't possible. Either change the subject matter of your attention—*what* you are thinking about—or change *how* you are thinking. Shift from negative thoughts to positive thoughts about the same subject.

> If you want a good relationship, give it positive attention.

Examples:

1. Changing the subject matter: "We sure are fighting a lot lately" to "When we make special time to be lovers, it is so beautiful."

2. Changing from thinking negatively to thinking positively about the same thing: "I don't see how I could ever forgive him for that" to "I know I can find the inner strength, the kindness and generosity, to forgive him if I really want to."

3. Changing from thinking about what you don't want to thinking about what you *do* want: "I don't want to argue" into "I want to have productive discussions with my mate."

After making it through one day, tackle the next in the same disciplined manner. Inspire yourself. How many days can you generate predominately positive thoughts about only what you *do* want? As you exercise your Mind Freedom, you will notice differences in your life:

1. The quality of your experiences will be quickly transformed.

2. You will begin to get more of what you *do* want.

The Discipline of Conscious Intention

Loose your imagination to create a vision of the kind of relationship you want. As you construct your vision, identify and focus on qualities of your relationship rather than characteristics of your partner. For instance, "I want a relationship that is full of laughter, honesty, and sensuality" rather than "I want a partner who is funny, truthful, and sexy," or "I want a relationship that is financially strong" rather than "I want a rich partner." Qualities of a relationship are much larger and more encompassing than either partner's individual traits. Your partner does not make it happen for you—you are *both* responsible for creating a well-balanced union.

Focus not on characteristics of partners but on qualities of a relationship.

Whenever you think about your relationship, concentrate on your vision. Choosing your vision, thinking about only what you *do* want, does not mean deceiving yourself about the state of your life. Be completely honest about what is going on in your life right now. If your actual relationship is unlike your vision, if you have relationship difficulties, as almost everyone does, compare them against your relationship vision and say to yourself, "I choose to have my relationship vision." Follow these steps:

1. *Compare* your current situation with your vision.

2. Consciously *choose* to have your vision.

3. Always *end your thinking* with your vision—the image of what you want.

Example:

Vision: an intimate, passionate, fulfilling sex life

Current situation: infrequent sex, sometimes great, sometimes satisfactory, sometimes unsatisfactory

Choice: a thoroughly satisfying sex life

Vision: an intimate, passionate, fulfilling sex life

Although creating and focusing on a relationship vision is a powerful way to unleash your Mind Freedom, remember that you must also act. Ensure that your actions support your vision, bringing you closer to what you want rather than erecting obstacles to keep you from it. Saying yes to a relationship implies that you will take responsibility to learn, to grow, to change, and to act in spite of emotional discomfort. With such conscious intention, your relationship becomes a crucible for confronting all of your personal/spiritual growth quandaries. Your issues come to the fore so that you can work through them to healing and freedom. This is essential if you are to become fit for a relationship and to have the happiness you desire. Resist laziness and reluctance, and get busy.

Developing Perspective and Celebrating Differences

Invite your witness consciousness to explore what you'd like to heal through your relationship practice. Stand back when you are involved in some activity and watch yourself as if you were a character in a movie. What are you doing right now? Why and how are you doing it? Pay attention to the motivations and patterns behind your actions. For instance, the next time you find yourself in a heated discussion with your mate, call on your observer to take a close look at what's really going on. Are you steaming ahead into a quarrel because the issue itself is really important to you? Or are you pushing your point because you really want to be in control, not just in this situation but in most?

Soon you will be able to recognize your own thought habits, such as "Oh, right now I'm in my worrying mode," "Mmm, here is my loving state," "Yikes, I'm taking a wanting-to-be-right stance," or "Aha, this is my conciliation manner." You will no longer be on automatic pilot, operating from sleepy old patterns, but will awake to choices and to the freedom that choice brings. By engaging your witness consciousness, you expand your capacity to eliminate your damaging behaviors and to amplify your constructive ones.

Use the power of your observer to recognize that your mate is your mirror. A partner acts as a mirror by reflecting back your own less-than-stellar traits, so you can polish them up, and by helping you find aspects of yourself that are lying hidden and undeveloped and waiting to be brought to light.

In the first instance, you might psychologically project onto your partner, blaming his or her deficiencies for your problem. However, by employing your witness consciousness, you might well find that irritation with your mate often roots in dissatisfaction with yourself. Your partner's traits that are bothering you right now are doing so because you're unhappy with your own frailties. Observe and name this projection, and turn that piercing gaze inward to make changes where they are really needed.

At the outset of a romance, partners are attracted by their opposing characteristics as well as by their similarities. The shy wallflower falls for the playful extrovert, the spendthrift is attracted to the financial planner, and the risk taker swoons for the cautious considerer. Your higher consciousness looks in the relationship mirror and recognizes these differences as opportunities to bring forth new aspects of yourself, to become more than past experience and learned behaviors have so far led you to be. However, your ego might fall into the romantic shadow trap of "I have found my other half. My lover, who is so different from me, completes me." The opportunity for growth is lost, and, after a certain period of time, because there has been no self-expansion but rather a contraction through dependency, those differences begin to lose their appeal.

Whether it is from fear of losing control of your partner, from uncertainty of your own beliefs, from a need to win or to be right always, or because of a host of other reasons, you

Take a look at things from your partner's perspective.

might start to complain about your partner's differences and demand changes. Rather than wanting your lover to be more like you, use your witness consciousness to step into your partner's shoes. Partners must allow each other room to breathe and to be. Ask "What can I learn from how she thinks about this?" rather than "Why doesn't she just agree with me?" Consider "What benefits are there in his approach to this situation?" instead of "I wish he'd learn to do it my way." Celebrate and learn from your differences. You'll see with new eyes and a broader viewpoint. Your relationship will flourish, retaining its spark and passion over the years.

Transforming Your Relationship

When you turn the keys of Mind Freedom, you unlock the potential for a truly satisfying union. By paying positive attention to your relationship, focusing on the qualities you want it to exhibit and seeing your part in its evolution, you can break free from limited societal models and forge a bond that is your own creation, uniquely and satisfyingly yours.

Use your Mind Freedom to help transform some of the common relationship fallacies that you are subtly and overtly bombarded with every day.

Transform: "One partner is responsible for taking care of the relationship, and the other is responsible for finance and practicalities of the world."

Into: "Both partners share responsibility for relationship success and for worldly necessities."

Transform: "A relationship is such a basic thing that I should know how to do it—there's something wrong with me/you if we don't know how."

Into: "Nobody starts out knowing how to do a relationship; it requires lifelong learning."

Transform: "A satisfying relationship is based on the right characteristics of the partners."

Into: "A satisfying relationship is based on the qualities of the relationship itself, which we are equally responsible for creating together."

Transform: "Commitment to a relationship means the end of freedom."

Into: "Commitment to a relationship provides me with an opportunity to heal myself and thus become truly free."

When you make choices with attention, intention, and awareness, you will discover that your creativity knows no bounds. Reach for your dream and you will unleash resources you did not know you had. In response to the challenge of manifesting your choices, you will develop your knowledge and skill, you will soar beyond all previous limits, and you will unlock the power of synchronicity whereby the universe and God come to your assistance in astonishing ways. You can have all that you want—true happiness, material abundance, vibrant health, and enduring love.

THE THIRD FREEDOM: *heart*

Essence of Emotion

Poets, mystics, philosophers, and scientists have long pondered the mysteries of the heart. Religious thought claims the heart as the center of spiritual love. Christianity associates divine love with the Sacred Heart of Jesus, Hindus revere Shiva's sacred heart, Buddhists extol the heart as the site of compassion, and Sufis see the heart as the seat of God. The ancient Egyptians believed that the heart was home not only to emotions but also to thought, personality, moral awareness, and the soul. Greek philosopher Aristotle believed that the heart, not the brain, was the seat of mental processes.

We now know that the heart does indeed have a mind of its own. Simple experiments on frogs in high school laboratories demonstrate that the heart, composed of involuntary cardiac muscle, is autogenic, or self-excitatory—signals for initiating contraction need not come from the brain but can also originate in the heart muscle itself.

Your heart beats continuously for your entire lifetime, fulfilling its primary function of circulating oxygen and nutrient-rich blood throughout your body. It also affects you in other ways: neurologically, by transmitting nerve impulses; biophysically, with pressure waves; biochemically, with hormones and neurotransmitters; and energetically, with electromagnetic fields. With every heartbeat, energy and information are transmitted to all

21

your cells and back again. This excited exchange is the energy charge we call *emotion* ("energy in motion"), from the Latin verb meaning "to move."[1]

Although your heart is about the size of your fist, metaphorically it can expand to embrace the entire planet and all humanity, as well as that one person who you know as your soul mate, in a sublime energy field of love and compassion. In order to expand your heart in this way, you must unlock it and reclaim your Heart Freedom.

Heart Freedom

The essence of heart is emotion. Heart Freedom enables you to experience a bountiful variety and complexity of feelings. The supreme emotion is love, which by its very nature implies a relationship, the lover and the beloved. In modern Western culture, couple relationships are often symbolized by the Valentine heart. If you both want to make your relationship work, pay attention to its heart, to the emotional, energetic, and spiritual connection between you. For relationship happiness, you must welcome, nourish, and cherish such deep connection.

The responsibility of Heart Freedom is to allow yourself to feel everything, both positive and negative, and to act despite your emotional discomfort. A few yogis claim they can voluntarily stop the heart from beating,[2] and who among us has not tried to deliberately stop our hearts from feeling? When the yogi stops his heart from beating, it is a demonstration of physical and spiritual mastery, but when you or I try to stop our hearts from hurting, it is only a pathetic kind of emotional suicide. If we try to turn our hearts off in order to be protected from feeling the pain of loss, abandonment, deceit, or betrayal, eventually we feel nothing at all and life becomes flat, dull, and boring. There is little pleasure, joy, or happiness, because we can't be fully human while trying to feel only the good things. With the heart, it seems to be "all or nothing at all."

Heart Freedom means feeling everything.

Hearts start out innocent and pure, loving spontaneously and unconditionally, but they become wounded through hurts and betrayals. We erect barricades to protect them against more pain. Your heart, however, longs to break out of its confinement and to return to the openness and freedom of its natural state. There's no freedom in a barricaded heart. Imposing isolation supports powerlessness, reinforces fear, and leads to physical and mental illness.

Healthy Emotions for Healthy Lives

A direct connection between your heart (emotion and feeling) and the rest of your body affects your state of health. Neurobiologist Candace Pert and a team of researchers with the National Institutes of Health (NIH) have identified "molecules of emotion." Combinations of tiny bits of protein on the surface of cells form receptors, sensors that collect chemical information carried throughout your body by other molecules called ligands. Receptors and ligands are very particular about the company they keep; to bind together, they must be perfectly matched. Some ligands are natural to the body, such as peptides, neurotransmitters, and hormones; some are natural but foreign to the body, such as viruses; others are artificial chemicals. When a ligand binds with a receptor (in what Pert calls "sex on a molecular level"[3]), information is deposited onto and into the receptor in a biochemical exchange that has profound effects. If a receptor waiting for a natural body ligand is unoccupied—because emotional repression has reduced the supply of peptides, for instance—a matching virus can dock, and illness results.

According to Dr. Pert:

> All emotions are healthy. . . . Anger, fear, and sadness, the so-called negative emotions, are as healthy as peace, courage, and joy. To repress these emotions and not let them flow freely is to set up a dis-integrity in the system, causing it to act at cross-purposes rather than as a unified whole. The stress this creates, which takes the form of blockages and insufficient flow of peptide signals to maintain function at the cellular level, is what sets up the weakened conditions that can lead to disease.[4]

In the 1940s, Wilhelm Reich was ridiculed for his assertion that failure to express sexual emotions caused cancer, but the receptor-ligand biochemical model lends credence to his theories. Although Reich did not know it, modern medical science recognizes that people have miniscule cancerous tumors developing within their bodies all of the time. Pert and her fellow researchers found that endorphins in the blood increased by 200 percent during sex.[5] It seems quite possible that when a person is sexually fulfilled, most of the receptors for cancer are occupied with endorphin ligands, so the disease can't develop further. The converse might also be true: if sexual emotions are repressed, endorphin ligands are absent and cancerous ligands can take their place.

Viruses and cancer aren't the only sicknesses that thrive on repressed emotion. Heart disease—now so pervasive that by the late 1960s the World Health Organization called it "the world's most serious epidemic"—loves emotional blocks. Of course, lifestyle choices (diet, exercise, smoking, and other physical stressors) are powerful contributors, but they are not the only culprits. Part of the problem stems from armoring our hearts against feeling too much, not allowing them to open fully to others. In his empowering book *Love and Survival: The Scientific Basis for the Healing Power of Intimacy*, Dr. Dean Ornish documents studies that conclude that intimacy (emotional support and connection) is at least as important as physical factors (such as cholesterol levels and blood pressure) for the prevention of and recovery from heart disease.[6]

Twelve Keys to the Kingdom of Your Heart's Desire

Thought cannot heal a broken heart, and thinking will never open a heart that is closed. Only feeling can accomplish such miracles. As Blaise Pascal said long ago, "The heart has its reasons which reason knows nothing of." The keys to healing and opening your heart can be found not in rationality but in the realms of emotion, energy, and spirit. You enter these mysterious domains through a relationship when you surrender fully to the joys and sorrows of giving and receiving love. In a truly committed relationship, you dare to start breaking open locks and knocking down walls.

Here are the keys necessary and sufficient to open every lock upon your heart:

Self-Love

Without self-love, there can be no love for another. Loving yourself is the secure foundation for all enduring relationships. Loving yourself keeps you going as long as there is hope of a breakthrough in a troubled relationship. Loving yourself gives you the courage to leave a bad relationship. It is the fountain from which flow your love, compassion, and generosity toward the soul mate you adore.

Intimacy

An intimate emotional, energetic, and spiritual connection with your lover will pick the mechanism of the trickiest lock. Sexual and spiritual ecstasy requires that the boundaries between you come down. Your armor must drop away. In a relationship, there is no other way to reach the highest joy. Real strength includes emotional vulnerability and the transparency of desire, allowing another person in to know all of you, including your perceived weaknesses as well as your strengths. Acting as if you are invulnerable, a mask designed to fool the world, is really only a self-delusion, like that of the man who wears a cheap toupee and assumes no one notices.

Commitment

Commitment is the determination to stand together through life's joys and sorrows, to maintain your vows of union, and to grow old together in love. It includes a willingness to avoid behaviors that threaten or endanger your relationship, particularly in sexual expression, which activates the emotional pitfalls of insecurity, fear, and jealousy. Commitment does not mean you cannot love any other, but it does mean that sexual love is exclusive to your chosen soul mate.

Selflessness

When acting selflessly, with your focus on others rather than yourself alone, you respect your partner and serve the larger world community. Selflessness stimulates empathy (the capacity to participate in another's emotions) and considers: "How will what I do or don't do affect the well-being of the one I love, of those closest to me, and of all others in this world?"

Kindness

Kindness, almost synonymous for love, is always unconditionally given without any expectations. How much have you dropped kindness from your behavior vocabulary with your lover? How much have your interactions become exchanges in which you give something only if there is a guarantee you'll receive something in return? When was your last random act of kindness toward your soul mate?

Daring

To be emotionally vulnerable, to make your fears, longings, and desires transparent, is to risk being judged, rejected, abandoned, and hurt. Daring to take such risks requires uncommon courage, especially if you have already been stung by betrayal. And yet there can be no open heart without risk taking.

Trust

Trust is a form of faith. In spite of past experiences of deceit or betrayal, you act to support your present relationship in love, kindness, and selflessness. You give and give some more, never counting the cost. You know that your actions will help bring out the very best in the one you love and that more love, more happiness, and more joy will come to both of you as well as to those around you.

Truth

It's true: the truth will set you free. You can't have the relationship you *do* want if you settle for one you don't want. Revealing your heart's desires to the one you love helps clear away the excess baggage of self-pity, suffering, doubt, and fear. Any relationship that cannot stand the truth will wither and die.

Unconditional Love

Like kindness, unconditional love acts without expectation of reward or result. You give just to give. Nevertheless, unconditional love does not mean that lovers don't help each other grow. You reject disrespect, abuse, or deceit. Unconditional love does not encourage you to stay in a really bad relationship. With unconditional love, you can love someone even if you don't like him. Moreover, you can love someone even if you can't stay in a relationship with her.

Forgiveness

Forgiveness is for you as much as for the one forgiven. You might not forget past transgressions, but you can gain the freedom to act as if they never happened. Forgiveness, however, is not blindness. You do not continue to accept the same hurtful behavior over and over again. You might be able to forgive someone who has harmed you, but you reject further mistreatment.

Pleasure

In a relationship, the giving of pleasure brings exquisite pleasure to the giver. Few things feel as good as completely pleasing your partner. Since giving and receiving pleasure are not only emotional acts but also spiritual ones, sensual and sexual pleasure can become gateways to spiritual awakening. Aren't you a better person when you regularly experience pleasure? According to neuropsychologist James Prescott, "Physical affectional pleasure is not only moral but is morally necessary if we are to become moral and spiritual persons in our common bond with humanity."[7]

Romance

Just as sensual nutrition is food for your Body Freedom, so is romance sustenance for your Heart Freedom. Romance simply involves repeatedly affirming how important your lover is to you. In the first heady days of falling in love, even the most unimaginative lover shows romantic behaviors. The trick of romance is to continue your amorous attentions after the early blush of romantic infatuation has faded.

Romance means making time for each other as lovers. Tell your mate how lovely she is. Assure your partner that you admire him. Small, affectionate tasks that require more effort than dollars (writing a poem or singing a love song) are just as much part of the lover's repertoire as big-ticket items like jewelry, candlelit dinners, and exotic vacations. Remember, the essential part is to recognize and demonstrate how important your relationship is to you.

Keys to your Heart Kingdom

Self-Love	Trust
Intimacy	Truth
Commitment	Unconditional Love
Selflessness	Forgiveness
Kindness	Pleasure
Daring	Romance

Men in a Relationship: The Hero Who Admits He Is Afraid

Many men are reluctant to embrace relationships, but relationships are the marquee event in the Olympics of life. Winning the gold medal in relationships is as good as it gets in this world. Ask yourself: Is a great relationship so rare because it is not worthy of my attention, or does my attention wander away from a relationship because of fear? Am I afraid of a relationship, or do I simply not know how to be in one? Fear and ignorance are two reasons why men resist intimacy and commitment so strongly.

To help men wholeheartedly embrace relationships, it is time to join three archetypes that have traditionally been separate: the hero, the warrior, and the lover. As Joseph Campbell said, "What's made up in the head is the fiction. What comes out of [the heart] is a myth. These are totally different things altogether."[8] What's made up in the head is the Hollywood hero—a heroic warrior-savior/destroyer. What can come out of the heart is a heroic warrior-lover.

The hero myth has been saturated by Hollywood with characters of extraordinary physical powers who are basically alone in life. They might have sexual relationships, but without emotional intimacy. If they are involved in love relationships, such relationships are viewed as liabilities, bringing an unwanted vulnerability to their characters and their circumstances. Although there are many images of the heroic warrior, there are few of the heroic lover. And the heroic warrior-lover is virtually nonexistent.

Like it or not, Hollywood is now the main source of our mythological incarnations. Few read the classics or ancient mythologies today. There are many Hollywood images of horrific warriors of destruction, such as Darth Vader, the Borg, the Terminator, and Sauron. Countering these demonic warriors are the heroic warriors who defeat them: Luke Skywalker, Captain Picard, Sarah Connor, Gandalf, and Aragorn. The heroic warriors who conquer evil using violence are rarely portrayed as lovers with lasting relationships. Now the time is ripe for warrior-lovers who conquer with love but remain lovers in the flesh.

Mahatma Gandhi and Dr. Martin Luther King are modern examples of warriors based in the unconditional love of nonviolence. They were remarkably courageous but essentially sexless in their public personas, perpetuating the unnecessary separation of sex and spirit typical of virtually all cultures of the world. A healthy, passionate sexuality is a natural human element connected to the universe's energy flow, which is fundamentally sensual and broadly sexual—penetration and envelopment in harmony and balance, the oneness of yin and yang. Denying the energy of eros, sensuality, and sexuality might be commendable if such denial were a necessary condition for spiritual awakening, but no one has ever convincingly demonstrated this is actually the case. Indeed, Tantric, Taoist, and Egyptian sacred sexuality practices have apparently been successfully employed as paths to enlightenment for thousands of years.

A number of recent observers have noted the connection between sexual repression, scarcity of pleasure, and increased violence. Here are two separate comments:

> A recent interview on National Public Radio with journalist Jonathan Rauch, who managed to enroll in an Islamic training school for future Jihad "warriors," suggests that the extreme sexual repression of these young men and boys results in what Rauch calls "a lust for death"—a transfer of libido that Freud would certainly have understood. All of which leaves war and those who participate in it looking like regressed juveniles at their animalistic worst.[9]

> Among human beings, a pleasure-prone personality rarely displays violence or aggressive behaviors, and a violent personality has little ability to tolerate, experience, or enjoy sensuously pleasing activities. As either violence or pleasure goes up, the other goes down.[10]

In elements of popular culture such as the cinema, superheroes are rarely associated with mature, fulfilling sexual relationships. However, they can be and should be. Doing so would begin the process of popularizing a model worthy of emulation: the hero as warrior and lover, all rolled into one glorious human being. The contribution this shift in attitude could make toward the well-being of humanity in general, and for personal happiness in particular, is extremely significant. The heroic warrior-lover is a worthy replacement for the lonely Hollywood warrior-savior/destroyer.

Superhero stories usually include the following powerful human qualities: overcoming extreme hardships, winning in spite of numerous setbacks and defeats, valiant actions in selfless service to others, extreme courage in the face of incredible threats, taking risks against impossible odds, kindness to strangers, and miraculous abilities. Warrior-lovers need to display degrees of these qualities if their relationships are to flourish. The primary task of the relationship superhero is not to seek out evil and destroy it, nor to dispense justice, but rather to enter unreservedly into a covenant of love. As Joseph Campbell states, "Where we thought to slay another, we shall slay ourselves; where we had thought to travel outward, we shall come to the center of our own existence; where we had thought to be alone, we shall be with all the world."[11]

Your challenge: become a heroic warrior-lover.

James Carse, professor of the history and literature of religion, differentiates between finite and infinite games. A finite game is competitive. Its purpose is to win—implying that there is one winner, everyone else loses, and then the game ends. On the other hand, infinite games are cooperative. Their purpose is to continue playing indefinitely, and every player is a winner. Competitive finite games focus on the end result, attaching little value to the playing of the game itself. Such games can become very nasty. Cooperative infinite games focus on the unfolding play—the journey is more important than the final destination. These games generate experiences of deep connection and intense feelings of love, devotion, and happiness.[12]

Most board games, card games, and sports games, such as Monopoly, poker, and baseball, are finite games. Life activities (games in our terminology) that involve ongoing interactive relationships, like marriage and business, can be played as either finite or infinite according to the preferences of the players. The nature of the relationships, not the structure of most life games, determines if they are finite or infinite. One notable exception is that most finite of all finite games, the game of war, in which one party must vanquish the other. There's no other way to play the game of war. One's only option is whether to play the game or not.

In life games, if the nature of the relationship is primarily competitive, it's likely to be finite. If the nature of the relationship is primarily cooperative, the game will more likely be played as infinite. When marriages work, they are splendid infinite games wherein both partners strive to create love for a lifetime together, such as in the movie *The Notebook,* starring James Garner and Gena Rowlands. When marriages don't work, they can rank among the nastiest of finite games, as in the film *The War of the Roses*, with Michael Douglas and Kathleen Turner.

The warrior-lover is certainly a winner, adept at playing both types of games and winning them all, but because his intimate relationships are treated as infinite cooperative games, both parties win, and the games can go on for a lifetime. Hence, the mature warrior-lover is not only at ease with commitment, monogamy, and intense lifelong relationships, he is also a master of the skills needed to create them.

Joseph Campbell describes two essential levels of myths: the local socializing myth and the universal archetypal myth. Although the local socializing myth ties us closely together with others in our families and community, it often excludes all those outside that community. The universal archetypal myth, on the other hand, connects us to all life on the planet and beyond into a mystical cosmos.[13] The heroic warrior-lover walks in both worlds. He opens his heart to join intimately with all other human beings in respect and tolerance, while at the same time he bonds with one other human being—his life partner—in sublime sexual union. The combined heroic warrior-lover is an archetype for the complete man and woman—the apex of human possibility. There can be no higher aspiration, no greater accomplishment, no more urgent transformation to ensure survival of planet Earth.

Keeping Your Heart Open

As you proactively manifest Heart Freedom, in the context of a monogamous committed relationship, your burden of fear, pain, and insecurity declines continuously and sometimes dramatically. You can heal wounds from childhood to the present quite naturally without extensive analysis. Reclaiming your Heart Freedom as you integrate all Four Freedoms brings about your healing.

It really is that simple, despite how serious you might think your emotional and relationship issues are. By opening your heart, you shift from a situation in which your past is powerful and you are powerless to one in which you are powerful and negative experiences from your past are powerless to influence your life now. Remember, the responsibility of the heart is to allow you to feel everything, both positive and negative. To keep your heart open, you must act to support creating the relationship you want in spite of emotional discomfort. Acting merely to feel better—that is, avoiding emotional and psychological discomfort—sabotages your Heart Freedom. There can be no opening of your heart without the willingness to become emotionally transparent and vulnerable. You must dare to risk feeling the pain and discomfort of rejection, judgment, abandonment, and any other negative state you might

Dare to become emotionally transparent.

dread. Taking these risks, daring to have faith in the one you love and who loves you, is where freedom and healing reside. While there is no guarantee that your relationship will last forever in happiness, an open heart is your best chance to create the relationship happiness you seek.

Heartbreak as Teacher

In your quest for Heart Freedom, there is value in the pain of a broken heart. It gives you feedback to learn about changing and growing. Pain can be seen not simply as arbitrary suffering, but as a teacher. Emotional discomfort and pain are inevitable parts of the human experience, but suffering is a dysfunctional overreaction. It is a choice you make, albeit unknowingly, to extend and add to your pain. Ironically, suffering is usually brought on by behaviors designed to avoid feeling pain—behaviors that keep your heart lonely and tightly locked. If you wish to surpass suffering and instead use the pain of heartbreak to grow into love, then dare to shift some of your misperceptions about affairs of the heart.

Change from: "People fall in love and live happily ever after—their hearts, once opened, stay that way."

Change to: "We can create love for the rest of our lives, but we must re-open our hearts every time they close. We must feed our relationship by spending lovers' time together. We must not take each other for granted."

Transform: "If you love me, you should know what I want."

Into: "Love requires a transparency of desire. I dare to risk making myself vulnerable by asking my lover for what I need and want."

Alter: "If you love me unconditionally, you'll accept everything I do."

To become: "I can separate loving my partner from blindly accepting hurtful behaviors."

Let go of: "I'll be saved and taken care of. Our relationship is a remedy for my weakness, a deliverance from neediness, an escape from powerlessness."

Keep: "A relationship requires courage and daring. It is a supreme achievement, a heroic journey, a challenge that I can rise to, that can bring out the best in me."

THE FOURTH FREEDOM: *soul*

One and All

You are a soul that has a body, not a body that has a soul. At first glance this might seem a petty semantic difference, but on further consideration the difference is profound. Instead of being a body with a soul trapped inside that longs to escape back to the One, the All, the Source, as a soul inhabiting a body you remain part of the All. Your soul connects you to everything because it *is* everything. Soul takes on material reality by joining with an individual body, mind, and heart. In the words of Candace Pert, "We are each of us an individual nodal point, each an access point into a larger intelligence . . . [that] big psychosomatic network in the sky."[1]

There is another way to express this. According to philosopher Alan Watts, "The universe *eyes* in the same way that a tree *apples*."[2] Each of these *eyes* is an *I*—an individual point of consciousness. The word *Soul* can be employed in a way similar to Watts's use of the term *universe*. In this terminology, the Soul *eyes*. We are what the Soul is doing. We all come out of Soul and return to it after the death of our bodies.

Essence of Soul

Soul is eternal, changeless, boundless, all-encompassing, whole, and perfect. All of existence is contained within time and space, but Soul does not exist in the same way that bodies or buildings or molecules exist. Rather, Soul simply *is*. Soul is outside the limitations of time and space. In order to communicate about Soul, we must use words, but Soul is not readily reducible to a verbal description. Such discussions entail the distinction between *a soul* and *the Soul*. While it is useful to talk about a soul as if each of us has one that is somehow separate from others, this is only a convenience, not an accurate description. The soul that inhabits our bodies, encompassing our hearts and minds, is the Soul. There is only one Soul, and we are all it. Ralph Waldo Emerson named it the "Over-soul, within which every man's particular being is contained and made one with all other . . . [and] the act of seeing and the thing seen, the seer and the spectacle, the subject and the object, are one."[3] However, our ordinary consciousness conceives and perceives dualistically, separating each material thing from all other material things, and each idea from all other ideas. Many philosophic and religious systems (for example, Zen Buddhism and Adviata Vedanta) suggest that the apparent separation is really an illusion, temporarily hiding the unity of all things.

The Soul is eternal, changeless, boundless, all-encompassing, whole, and perfect.

Soul is the primary life force that contains, connects, and animates everything. Metaphorically speaking, Soul is like air. You can separate a quantity of air from a body of air, but when you return the air that was separated, there is only one body of air. Separation exists in Body, Mind, and Heart Freedom, but not in Soul Freedom. Soul's desire is to manifest union in the material realm, to rejoin that which has been arbitrarily separated, to bring into synchronicity and harmony all Four Freedoms—Body, Mind, Heart, and Soul. As Novalis said in *Hymns to the Night*, "The seat of the soul is there, where the outer and the inner worlds meet." While there are many paths to the meeting place of inner and outer worlds, of spirit and matter, a mate relationship is one of the most readily available and easily accessible. It is the primary vehicle through which human beings can join together and, in doing so, create union. Your relationship can become your spiritual practice. Through its joys and trials, you can learn to become the best you can be.

Soul Freedom

The essence of Soul Freedom is faith. Science is what you believe because of the evidence. In spiritual matters, faith is what you believe despite evidence to the contrary. Faith enables you to keep going when all appears hopeless and to say, "That can't be all the evidence." With faith, you know that however bad the current situation might be, something better is just around the corner. Cynicism is the opposite of faith. The cynic knows that nothing will turn out well, no matter how good things are right now. However fashionable and humorous cynicism might be, ultimately it will drag you down, while faith will lift you higher and higher.

When you are in a relationship centered in Soul Freedom, you have faith that you can create a passionate, harmonious life with your mate even though couples around you might be leading lives of stressed dullness and disconnection. You have faith that together you can weather the storms that life will rain on you and that your relationship can be the rock to keep you safe above the flood.

The Responsibility of Soul Freedom

Faith and cynicism are both choices. Which choice you make determines the quality of your life and the state of your happiness. Choosing faith is itself a leap of faith. This is true alchemy, whereby you literally create something from nothing—there was no faith, then there is. The responsibility of Soul Freedom is to choose faith.

Having faith doesn't mean you sit back and do nothing. On the contrary, the responsibility of Soul Freedom includes the necessity to take action. At the same time, you let go of attachment to the results of your action. You turn the final outcome and how it unfolds over to that which is much larger than yourself (God, Goddess, the Divine). But as this old story shows, choosing faith is not always easy:

> A cloistered monk is walking along the edge of a cliff during his morning meditation. He slips over the edge but stops himself from falling to certain death on the rocks hundreds of feet below by grabbing onto a small bush whose roots are barely clinging to the cliff face. As he hangs precariously, he shouts, "Is anybody up there?" Immediately, a booming voice replies, "Yes, I am. It's God. You'll be fine, just let go of the bush." The monk reflects for a second and replies, "Is anybody *else* up there?"

Surrender

The challenge and opportunity of faith is to surrender to God's will (the divine rhythm, the flow of the Tao), believing that however badly things might be going in this moment, in the long term you will attain your heart's true desire and your life will unfold in a way that is better than you could possibly have imagined, planned for, or created with your personal willpower. To live in a state of faith and surrender is to reclaim your Soul Freedom. As with the dangling monk, you reclaim your Soul Freedom by answering the call to let go of the bush.

Choose faith and take action.

Imagine that you don't speak the same language as God. How could God then communicate with you? Perhaps God would close some doors and at the same time open others. You would be guided to find the right path—a path of self-actualization and service to the world. When a door closes, it can seem like setback, failure, or defeat. Sometimes it will be catastrophic or tragic, for example, when you lose a loved one. But what will you learn from the experience? How will your character develop in response to it? How will your spirit awaken? How will it affect your ability to give and receive love? How will it affect your ability to stay present moment by moment? And how will you grow in wisdom? Your attitude toward adversity changes dramatically when you frame it in these spiritual terms. Consider that God may shake the world so that which is unshakable will be revealed.

We don't always recognize or agree with God's way of opening and closing doors. Our vision is narrow, and we only see what we want to see or expect to see, just like the man in this modern fable:

> A man is trapped in his house by a flood. As the waters rise, he goes out onto his porch. Someone comes by in a rowboat and offers to take him to safety. But the man says, "No, thanks. God will provide for me." The waters continue to rise rapidly. The man goes out onto his second-story balcony. Someone comes by in a speedboat and offers to take him to safety, but the man says, "No, thanks. God will care for me." The waters continue to rise, and the man crawls onto his roof, the only place left to go. A helicopter comes by and the crew urges the man to board and be taken to safety, but he says, "No, thanks. God will protect me." That night, the man drowns. When he comes face to face with his Creator, the man says, "I thought you were going to take care of me!" God replies, "I sent two boats and a helicopter. What more could I do?"

Let go of your expectation of the outcome. When you catch yourself focused on a particular outcome, making judgments about how something is unfolding, try to let go and simply be with what is, while keeping an eye open for the silver lining in even the worst scenario. This could be a radical departure from how you are currently living, but it opens the doorway for you to consider the possibility that something horrible now might be a wonderful and essential part of your spiritual growth, speeding you along the path to your highest self.

Surrender is more easily done by action than by analysis. Instead of thinking about "Why is this happening? What is the meaning of life?" ask instead, "How can I act to make my life meaningful?" Your answer is to live a life of passionate detachment.

Passionate Detachment

Carlos Castaneda has written a series of remarkable books in which he describes his sha-manic apprenticeship with the Yaqui sorcerer Don Juan. Don Juan advises Castaneda that a man of knowledge (an impeccable warrior) chooses a path and follows it with heart, acting as if what he does matters, even though he knows that it does not, and understanding that nothing is more important than anything else.[4]

Passion acts with great enthusiasm, extraordinary intensity, and deep feelings. Detach-ment lets go of all concern for the results of the action. Upon first consideration, it might seem as if passion and detachment don't belong together. You might conclude that if you were detached you would not feel strongly about a situation, but would be indifferent and feel little or nothing. Detachment without passion, a boring dullness of caring about nothing, is a dreadful state of consciousness. No wonder so few have chosen detachment as a serious spiritual practice.

When Don Juan advises to "act as if what you do matters," he is suggesting action with passion. When you act with passion, you feel truly, completely alive. This is because pas-sion exists only in the now moment—you feel passion now or not at all. On the other hand, detachment is about the future. Detachment means you completely surrender and let go of your concern for the future outcome of your action. You are not detached about the action itself. On the contrary, you are filled with passion in the now moment.

Detachment flows naturally from the wisdom of acknowledging Don Juan's advice that "nothing matters more than anything else." What you do does not really matter in the sense that ultimately you have no control over anything. Outcomes or results might not be any-thing like what you intend them to be. All you have is choice about what you will do and how you will be in the now moment. You are able to let go of concern for the results of your actions because you understand that each individual is a tiny part of something infi-nitely vast and wonderful that you can influence but cannot control.

When you understand that you have control over nothing, your response can be despair or detachment. Despair is powerless, while detachment is a quality of Soul Freedom. Soul knows you don't need control. All is as it should be. Your life is unfolding as part of a grand cosmic natural order. You fit into that larger natural order whether you want to or not and whether you are aware of it or not. Your challenge and opportunity is to say yes to what is—all of it, exactly as it is, for better or worse, right here, right now.

It is a paradox that making choices can both bring freedom to you and rob you of it. That you can make choices is the chief characteristic of all freedom, but if you are attached to the outcomes of your action, you lose freedom as soon as you obtain it. You become a slave to your choices, stuck in a self-constructed rut. If you worry about the results of your actions, you are robbed of the natural joy of being fully present in the now moment. However, by making choices, by acting with passion, and by being detached from the results of your actions, you remain completely free. You act boldly without taking yourself too seriously.

In your relationship, passionate detachment means putting the best of yourself into your life together. Allow your creativity to shine forth in your actions, to reveal your love, respect, and desire, but without expectation of your mate's response. You might plan to be together forever and do your best to make that happen, but you know that you have no real control over the future—accident, illness, or adversity can separate you. Nevertheless, don't let that stop you from committing to a lifetime of loving.

The Meaning of Life and the Meaning in Life

The meaning *of* life is forever a mystery. Some mysteries are unsolvable and best left that way. But the meaning *in* life is entirely different. Life is not a problem needing a solution; it is an experience to be lived fully in the present, moment by moment. Meaning is not built into the actions, events, or outcomes you encounter in your life. On the contrary, you bestow meaning upon them as an act of your Soul Freedom. In this sense, something is only as important as you determine it to be. Because experience is so subjective, it is primarily your beliefs and emotions that determine how you bestow meaning. Different people attach different meanings to the same thing.

You bestow the meaning in life.

When people forget that the meaning they bestow upon something has real significance only for themselves, the result can be conflict not only on a grand scale but also in basic, everyday events. You might recognize these situations from your own relationship:

1. One of you stresses that it is essential to be early for appointments because being early *means* you are conscientious and thoughtful.

   The other prefers to arrive just as activities are getting underway because being early *means* you are uptight and trying to be in control.

2. One of you wants to spend money on a new luxury SUV because showing your affluence *means* you are successful.

   The other prefers to buy a standard-model vehicle because showing your affluence *means* you are materialistic and competitive.

Fortunately, beliefs and emotions are open to change, and by simply remembering that things mean what you determine them to mean, you and your partner don't have to choose one way or the other. You could agree to disagree and come to a solution not based primarily on a need for one of you to be right or for both of you to share a single point of view. You can create new ways from two ways.

Knowing that *you* bestow meaning enables you to elevate the simplest facets of your relationship to moments of great power and beauty. Examples:

- Giving meaning to your relationship by making it the most important thing

- Regarding your relationship as a spiritual practice

- Elevating your sex to sacred loving

- Transforming ordinary activities, such as bathing, preparing and eating food, dancing, and touching, into ceremonial and ritualized behaviors

- Treating every moment as a meditation

Ceremony and Ritual

Through ritual, ceremony, and energy practices, we touch the unknown and the unknowable—the divine mystery. Ritual and ceremony are the language of the soul. They activate the awesome, magical possibilities in the imaginative realm of our creativity. We are amazed, astonished, and filled with wonder. We are renewed. Such mystery is never knowable in advance, never predictable, and therefore never boring.

In ceremony and ritual, lovers see and treat each other as a god or a goddess, worthy of adoration. Looking for the divine in your partner enables you to become aware of the other's glory. You transcend the pathetic and pitiful worldview that insists humanity is corrupt and sinful. Ceremony and ritual reintroduce play and a delightful lightness of being into your relationship. Masks, costumes, candles, crystals, semiprecious stones, incense, and sweet grass are some of the tools used in ceremony and ritual. Let your imagination run wild.

Ritual is the soul's language.

Soul Sex

The spiritual quest does not have to be an isolated, lonely journey. In soul sex, lovers fly into the mystery together, inviting God into their hearts and into their beds. There is complete surrender to each other and to God. Hearts are made sweet by surrender to each other, and souls are made sweet by surrender to God. Control is the enemy of ecstasy. The more we try to keep things under control, the more we reveal our insecurity. Opening unconditionally to the wonder of what is and the mystery of what is yet to come is real freedom.

Soulful lovers join with God in divine mystical union. This is possible because we are spirits in a body. Each individual is a node of consciousness capable of merging with all and everything. As a drop of water merges into the sea, so are you capable—by your very nature—of knowing God through direct personal experience. Such an experience is a gift of grace, the manifestation of complete Soul Freedom.

Happiness

Happiness is your birthright. Happiness does not need to be a fleeting, momentary, and fragile thing. Happiness is a natural accompaniment to Soul Freedom. Soul finds happiness in simplicity, in the mystery of everyday life—the warmth of a lover's touch, the interplay of stimulating conversation, the satisfaction of a job done well together.

When you enter into a committed relationship with another human being, vowing a covenant with each other, you take a giant step in reclaiming your Soul Freedom. Happiness becomes free of the chains that bound it to the circumstances of your life. Your happiness is no longer dependent on whether your life situations are going well or badly. Such is the experience of transcendence that accompanies the embrace of Soul Freedom.

Embracing Soul Freedom keeps the longest-term relationship interesting, stimulating, ever-evolving, changing, and growing. Cultivating Soul Freedom helps carry you through difficult times in your relationship. Your body is easily damaged, your head is easily confused, and your heart is easily wounded, but Soul hangs in there through thick or thin, through the ups and downs, for better or worse.

To allow Soul Freedom to flourish in your relationship:

Unlearn: "I act according to the dictates of my emotions or the dictates of my mind."
Learn: "I listen to my higher self (Soul) for direction and guidance."

Unlearn: "Spirituality is separate from the rest of my life—from sex, from work, from shopping, and so on."
Learn: "My whole life is a meditation. Our relationship is a spiritual practice, and our lovemaking is a sacrament."

$\mathcal{J}$NTEGRATING YOUR
four freedoms

Everything is consciousness.

Daniel Odier,
Tantric and Chan master

Ultimate reality is a universal consciousness.

Richard Dolan,
mathematician

Love is the experience of unity. The demolition of walls, the fusion of two energies is what the experience of love is. Love is the ecstasy when the walls between two people crumble down, when two lives meet, when two lives unite. When such a harmony exists between two people I call it love. And when it exists between one man and the masses, I call it communion with God.

Osho,
From Sex to Superconsciousness[1]

Separation or Unity—What Is the Nature of Reality?

The Western world loves to compartmentalize, creating boxes of separation so that the complexities of life are easier to comprehend and simpler to cope with. We separate work from family life, spiritual practice from sexuality, social policy from corporate profit, and art from infrastructure. We manifest these divisions not only in society at large but also within ourselves, separating our minds from our hearts and our bodies from our souls.

Although there are many who have helped instill this pattern of separation, one of the most influential was the seventeenth-century French mathematician and philosopher René Descartes. Descartes divided everything into two mutually exclusive but interacting categories: *res cognitans* (the subjective realm of consciousness and thought) and *res extensa* (the objective realm of the material world). His distinction was very useful, clearing the way for science to progress rapidly, free of interference from the dogma of religious doctrine. However, since the time of Descartes, scientists considering consciousness have primarily explored it from the perspective of "Where does consciousness come from?" This question assumes that consciousness is dependent on or derived from something else, usually material reality. In addition, because science endeavors to be objective, focusing on the observable and measurable and avoiding the subjective, the study of consciousness (pure subjectivity) is often dismissed as outside the realm of natural science altogether, thereby perpetuating separation of mind and body.

Such separation orientation worked well under the old scientific models. There, at the macro level (a scale large enough to encompass galaxies), Isaac Newton's classical mechanics defined time and space as absolute. At the subatomic quantum level, matter (in the form of particles) and energy (as waves) were understood to be the tiny, distinct building blocks of physical reality. With the birth of quantum theory, and most recently string theory, this dualistic approach to reality no longer neatly fits. Modern physics is entering a phase that many of today's best scientists describe as "weird." Consider these examples:

- Matter can be converted into energy in nuclear reactors, and energy can be converted into matter in accelerators—they are interchangeable.

- Subatomic particles, through "superposition of states," can be in many states at once. Until an observer tries to measure the particle, it can be located anywhere and have any speed. It is only the act of observation that forces the particle to collapse into a particular state.[2]

- Through "quantum entanglement," the condition of one particle can influence the condition of another particle instantaneously at any distance.[3]

- All subatomic particles exhibit a property known as "wave-particle duality."[4] Inside the atom is the nucleus, inside the nucleus are protons and neutrons, and inside the protons and neutrons are quarks. When scientists want to study something too small to see even with the most powerful microscopes, they will often look for and record evidence that what they are studying leaves a trail behind. The trail left by particles (matter) is different from the trail left by waves (energy). However, this tiny thing they are observing will sometimes leave a trail as if it were a particle and at the next observation will leave a trail as if it were a wave. For example, light, most commonly assumed to be a wave, is also a particle (the photon), while electrons, generally considered particles, can also behave as waves. Whether something behaves like a wave or a particle depends on the observer and the type of observation. The observer and the observed cannot be arbitrarily separated, even for the convenience of the scientist attempting to remain objective.

String Theory

The theory of strings, sometimes referred to as the theory of everything,[5] is considered by many physicists to be the most promising explanation to date for the nature of ultimate reality. It suggests the possibility that there is a connection, as well as a separation, between the realms of the material and consciousness. Both conditions can exist at the same time.

According to physicist David Gross:

> There is about as complete unification as one could desire. Within this theory one is not saying that there are a few kinds of objects, and that everything else is built out of them. In some sense, we are saying that in string theory there is one object. . . . In the same way that if you take a violin string, and you pluck it, it has many kinds of vibrations. So, one violin string can give rise to many sounds. All of the tones of a vibrating string are different modes of one object. . . . That is true unification of everything, in that all the particles in the theory, and all the interactions, the particles that govern interactions, are all vibrations of the same string.[6]

In other words, a string is not a building block, as we have previously imagined particles to be. Apparently, the universe is not made by adding a bunch of strings together in different combinations to create all of the different things we observe, such as giraffes and people, buildings and stars. In Gross's view, there is only one string.[7]

If physical reality is not ultimately made out of matter, but rather vibrates out of something called a string, then it is possible that material reality and consciousness, rather than being dualistically separate, are instead intimately connected, affecting each other in mutual feedback loops. They not only have points at which they interact but are a single undivided system.

Remote-Viewing Experiments

Outside the realm of physics, other experiments have shown that there are connections between mind and matter that can't be explained by the old model of separation. Studies starting in 1972 and lasting over two decades were conducted under the sponsorship and supervision of the CIA and the United States Department of Defense. These experiments involved sets of two people who had no contact with each other. One person acted as a remote viewer while the other randomly selected a location to visit anywhere on the planet. Although the remote viewers had never physically been there, they accurately described the chosen sites. These tests illustrate that consciousness exists and operates across space.

Perhaps even more remarkable is that in another set of experiments, remote viewers accurately described the scene *before* the location was randomly selected. These studies demonstrate that consciousness exists and operates outside of both time and space.

According to H. E. Puthoff, the founding director of the remote-viewing research project at Stanford Research Institute in Menlo Park, California, "The integrated results appear to provide unequivocal evidence of a human capacity to access events remote in space and time . . . by some cognitive process not yet understood. . . . This fact must be taken into account in any attempt to develop an unbiased picture of the structure of reality."[8]

University of Oregon physicist Amit Goswami agrees. "Psychic phenomena, such as distant viewing and out-of-body experiences, are examples of the nonlocal operation of consciousness," he suggests. "Quantum mechanics undergirds such a theory by providing crucial support for the case of nonlocality of consciousness."[9]

If the difference between particles and waves is so slippery, and if time and space are so easily transcended, what is the fundamental nature of reality? What is real? One answer is *consciousness*. Consciousness is original and fundamental; everything considered to be "reality" comes out of that consciousness. In his book *The Self-Aware Universe*, Dr. Goswami presents a philosophical argument known as monistic idealism to explain his theory that both matter and mind have their origin in consciousness. He draws on the ancient Indian philosophy of Advaita Vedanta as his authority for using the term *consciousness* as "the Ground of All Being."[10]

Consciousness is fundamental.

As the foregoing examples illustrate, Western science is moving closer to Eastern perceptions of reality, wherein all is one. Body, mind, and spirit are not separate entities. Not only mystics but also an increasing number of scientists, philosophers, and medical doctors are talking openly about subtle energy, consciousness, and God. Candace Pert refers to subtle energy as "a still mysterious fifth force beyond the four conventional forces of physics . . . to scientifically explain anomalies such as the power of love."[11] And according to Robert Gottesman, M.D.:

> If information exists outside of the confines of time and space, matter and energy, then it must belong to a very different realm from the concrete, tangible realm we think of as "reality." And since information in the form of biochemicals of emotion is running every system of the body, then our emotions must also come from some realm beyond the physical. Information theory seems to be converging with Eastern philosophy to suggest that the mind, the consciousness, consisting of information, exists first, prior to the physical realm, which is secondary, merely an out-picturing of consciousness. . . . Consider that the body itself may be a metaphor, just a way of referring to an experience we all have in common. Maybe it's that we don't have consciousness, but consciousness has us.[12]

In the science, philosophy, medicine, and mysticism of the East, body, mind, heart, and soul are treated as inseparable and indivisible (non-dual). In the West, physicists, psychologists, and neurologists now largely agree that mind and body operate as a single system. From this perspective, the brain is just another organ, albeit more intricate than the rest of the body. Thoughts and emotions that subjectively bestow meaning on our reality are the result of complex electrochemical and biochemical interactions within and between cells throughout our body as well as in our brain. What happens in the body affects our minds and our hearts, and what takes place in the mind affects the body and the emotions in an endless series of feedback loops.

If science has come to see that we are not isolated elements but essentially one though inexplicable whole, isn't that inspiration for us to apply this same approach to ourselves and our lives? If everything is ultimately a unique vibration of one fundamental string, isn't it time for you to treat body, mind, heart, and soul as one undivided system?

Developing an Empirical Awareness of the Four Freedoms

You can do simple experiments to comprehend that all elements of you are interconnected.

1. For thirty seconds, think a very negative thought, for instance, that your partner has left you, that you have been fired, or that your home has burned down. Stop the thought and turn your attention to your feelings. What emotions have come up in you? Now focus on your body. Do you feel tension or pain anywhere? Notice that just one intense thought has affected your whole system.

2. Do some conscious emotional release. For thirty seconds, scream out loud, jump up and down, and roar out anger, pain, or sadness. Stop. Now put your attention into your body. Does it feel looser? Feel your energetic self. Do you feel a vibration, a lightness? How is your mind? Is it free and uncluttered? Note: Because we are taught to be very much "in control," the first time you do this you might have thoughts like "Uh-oh, I'm losing it" or "This is foolish," but if you pay attention to the effects emotional release has on you, those thoughts will dissipate.

3. Have a massage, either from your lover, a friend, or a professional massage therapist. As your body relaxes, notice how your emotions calm, your mind slows down, and you feel at peace and connected.

Living a Life of Pleasure

The true nature of reality is obviously a mystery. There is no "objective reality" to fasten onto as a conclusive guide for living. This can be frightening or freeing, for if there is no absolute certainty, then your reality is up to you. You create your reality through your concepts and belief system.

If you conceive of life as hard, people as self-serving, and yourself as a lone struggler amidst chaos, that is most likely the reality you will experience. If you conceive of life as an adventure, people as fellow travelers, and yourself as an explorer of the great unknown, that is most likely the reality you will experience, and so on through infinite possibilities and permutations. Your perception and experience will follow your belief no matter what the actual circumstances of your life situation.

One path to enlightenment is pleasure.

If you want a happy, balanced reality, allow yourself to cultivate a pleasure perspective. The enlightened master Osho taught that the clearest path to enlightenment is not through hardship but pleasure. Partake of pleasure; realize bliss.

Our culture manifests a dichotomy toward pleasure. On one hand we crave it, while on the other we deny it. Our body is designed for pleasure (for example, in the female body, the only purpose of the clitoris is pleasure). In the absence of pleasure, human beings can become crabby, mean, and physically or mentally ill. When regularly experiencing pleasure, most people are happier, nicer to be with, and more productive in their work. Nevertheless, we are taught that a worthy life is one of hard work and self-denial and that we should be satisfied with receiving our pleasure in the hereafter.

Some people confuse real pleasure with instant gratification. They become hedonists, acting only for immediate physical enjoyment and temporary emotional highs. Always seeking pleasure, always avoiding pain, a hedonist's life is shallow and ultimately unsatisfactory. Since our culture repeatedly warns us of the dangers of hedonism, it is a challenge to learn to accept pleasure. People fear doing so will make them bad, selfish, and greedy. However, adopting a pleasure orientation does not mean you become a hedonist. It does mean that you are grateful to be a spirit in a body. You feel all the joys and the sorrows of love and loss. You give thanks for each new day. You celebrate living. You play and work hard. You do your inner work to become fit for a relationship and to awaken spiritually. You understand that no one is always happy, but you also understand that your happiness is not dependent upon the changing circumstances of your life. You make happiness a choice, a way of living intentionally and consciously, and you can be content even in the face of adversity. You understand that pain is not optional (it's part of the human experience) but that suffering is unnecessary and avoidable. Adversity and pain become not your masters but your teachers.

When you adopt a pleasure orientation, you don't have to seek pleasure. It simply comes to you. When you enter into a committed relationship, when you open your heart to give and receive love, when you surrender and let go of all need to control everything, when you stay mindful (fully present from moment to moment), you will regularly experience great pleasure and know deep happiness.

Desire as Freedom

Just as we are sometimes taught that pleasure is a sinful path to follow, so are we warned of the terrible power of desire. Desire can lead us to overindulgence, to betrayal, and to misery.

"The abstinent run away from what they desire, but carry their desires with them. When a man enters reality, he leaves his desires behind him." So says Lord Krishna in the *Bhagavad-Gita*.[13] You can interpret this to mean that an awakened person no longer has any desire, or you can understand that it means he is not governed by desire. Desire exists, but in making his choices, he does not do so based on desire. He leaves desire behind. You can recognize desire as simply another element of life (like your thoughts, feelings, and physical sensations) and choose to act on your desires or not. You don't have to suppress them, but you know that you are not your desires and therefore are not ruled by them. You are not at the mercy of your passions.

On the contrary, desire provides motivation. Realizing the true desires of your heart is one of the great pleasures in life. Desire is fuel for healthy living. The freedoms of desire include:

- Desire for spiritual awakening

- Desire that supports you manifesting your vision

- Desire that supports fulfilling your purpose in your life

- Desire as passion and pleasure

The trap comes when you feel you *must* act on the desires you feel, particularly sexual desire. If you feel horny, you have to do something about it. Conversely, if you have no sexual desire, then you have no reason to engage in sexual activity. Conflict in relationships can occur when one partner has more sexual desire than the other. The lustier partner might pester the other for more sexual activity and, if it isn't forthcoming, might seek sexual satisfaction outside the relationship, feeling quite justified in doing so.

If, however, you can recognize desire as energy, just as emotions are, you can decide how to use that energy based on all your freedoms. Sexual energy is simply another form of life force energy. By perceiving desire as fuel for action, you can transform and use it for the highest self-actualization. Just as energy can be converted into matter and matter into energy, so too can you transform sexual desire into something else, such as emotional connection or creative inspiration. This is not suppression of your desires; it is transformation embedded in freedom. Such knowledge allows you to open without reservation into intimate emotional connection with more than just your chosen partner. It allows you to touch others with love, tenderness, and compassion without fearing it will lead to inappropriate sexual touching.

Desire is energy, fuel for life.

Knowing that you can transform sexual desire into emotional connection also empowers you to convert emotional connection into sexual passion, thereby overcoming problems of mismatches in sex drive. It can enable you to maintain a fulfilling sexual life to any age, despite hormonal changes that reduce libido, such as the decline of testosterone. You can begin lovemaking—you can even initiate it—without already being aroused. Skilled lovers who are emotionally open and energetically connected, with conscious mental focus and attunement to their bodies, know that passion will awaken as lovemaking progresses. Lovemaking becomes more than just a release of sexual tension; it becomes a meditation.

Tantric, Taoist, and Egyptian sacred sex practices regard lovers' sexual union as a physical expression of the highest consciousness in which all Four Freedoms integrate seamlessly. For example, Tantras are commentaries on the dialogues between the Hindu god Shiva and his consort Shakti, the masculine and feminine aspects of the same deity. When they make love, they merge as one and all life flows from their sacred embrace. "All the Universe is the play of Sakti-Siva. Sakti is Siva, and Siva is Sakti."[14]

Yoga means "union." Tantric yoga is a direct route to the unity of being, a realization of God Consciousness. As Tantric and Chan (Chinese Zen) master Daniel Odier says, "Pure happiness is the non-differentiation between the Tantric practitioner and the universe."[15] In this awakened state of illumination, ordinary sex is elevated to the level of sublime spiritual bliss, something far beyond the simple pursuit of pleasure or enhanced orgasms. According to the teachings of Chan master Houei-hai, "If you create duality, that's ordinary passion. Sacred passion springs from an absence of all duality."[16]

Integration in Mate Relationships

A mate relationship is a superlative setting for integrating your Four Freedoms. A relationship is the ideal arena for learning to become whole. Lovers do not complete each other but rather compose one whole relationship. Not only is a committed relationship a testing ground for confronting issues of personal and spiritual growth, but it also provides a secure haven in which to do so. In its cocoon, you can cultivate pleasure and explore desire.

One of the most powerful choices you can make on your path to total freedom is to select your relationship as the most important thing in your life. When you make this choice, your relationship becomes a spiritual practice. Three essential qualities of a relationship as spiritual practice are commitment, fidelity, and time. In a relationship covenant, commitment affirms your intention to grow old together. Monogamy provides the security you need to risk being emotionally vulnerable and transparent, so you can open the door to a shared sexual/spiritual ecstasy. Spending lovers' time together feeds the relationship through such simple activities as daily gazing into each other's eyes, sending love back and forth, and taking a weekly block of hours to be lovers.

As you engage in the intimacies of your relationship, as you learn the knowledge and skills to become fit for a relationship, you will naturally call upon, activate, and reinforce your Four Freedoms. No matter how irrelevant or frightening a particular freedom can seem, it is essential to embrace each of them, because they all interact subtly in an infinite number of ways. Synchronizing, integrating, and bringing the Four Freedoms (Body, Mind, Heart, and Soul) into harmony are some of the most important tasks you can possibly undertake. Your health, well-being, and happiness depend upon harmonization. The Four Freedoms are optional, not mandatory. It is your responsibility to reclaim and embrace these freedoms.

Embrace all of your Four Freedoms.

Reclaiming your Four Freedoms is not particularly difficult. You do not have to search to find them, for they reside within you. You do not have to earn them, because they are your birthright. You do not have to deserve them, because they wait to be claimed in the lost-and-found room where you have forgotten that you left them.

The essence of Body Freedom is direct sensory experience of what you see, hear, taste, smell, and touch in the now moment. To reclaim Body Freedom, adopt a pleasure orientation. Touch, make love, learn the art of sacred sex, and set aside shame associated with your body, sex, and experiencing pleasure. Love yourself, love your mate, love life.

The essence of Mind Freedom is consciousness. The responsibility of Mind Freedom is to exercise two kinds of choices. The first is *what* you think about: your attention. The second is *how* you think: your intention. You can choose to pay attention to what you *do* want rather than what you don't want. The subject of your attention becomes a choice—you are saying that you want more of it. You can think about what you want in a consistently positive way. Then you must take action to support your thoughts.

The essence of Heart Freedom is emotion, the capacity to feel. The supreme emotion is love, which by its very nature implies a relationship, the lover and the beloved. The responsibility of Heart Freedom is to allow yourself to feel everything, both positive and negative, and, in addition, to act in spite of emotional discomfort. Your challenge is to repeatedly open your heart every time it closes.

The essence of Soul Freedom is faith. In spiritual matters, faith is what you believe even in spite of evidence to the contrary. With faith, you know that however bad the current situation is, something better is just around the corner. The responsibility of Soul Freedom includes the necessity to take action in faith, regardless of how hopeless the situation might appear.

Vision and Purpose

Choice is the foundation of all Four Freedoms. You reclaim your freedoms by making new choices and acting consistently to support those choices. Although you won't get what you want if you don't know what it is, you don't have to know *exactly* what you want before you get started along your path. Your vision becomes clear, and your purpose in life will reveal itself to you if you are making choices, taking action, and learning from your mistakes. Your first step along the path to total freedom is to consciously embrace and reclaim your Four Freedoms. Rereading the first part of this book will help you, but doing the exercises will make a greater impact.

Think carefully about what the Four Freedoms are, and then *make a conscious choice* to fully integrate them into your daily living. Write the names of the Four Freedoms on a sticky note and post it where you will see it. Every day, repeat aloud one or more of the affirmations below (or your own versions) as a guide to help you manifest your freedom.

I choose to live, to awaken, to evolve, to be free.

I choose **Body Freedom**.
    I love my body.
    My body is naturally beautiful just as it is now.
    My body is the sacred temple for Soul.
    Pleasure is good. Sex is good.
    I open to all of the glorious senses by which I can know the world.
    I will touch my lover today.

I will ask for what I want from my lover.

I will take care of my body so it remains healthy.

I choose **Mind Freedom**.

I have the power over what I think about and how I think about what I think about.

I will think only about what I *do* want. I will consistently think about what I want in a positive way.

I will think about freedom, success, abundance, happiness, love, health, and peace.

I will act to support myself in moving closer to my vision.

I will bring my vision into alignment with my purpose in life by following my bliss. I will do what I love to do.

I choose **Heart Freedom**.

I give thanks to be alive.

Thank God(dess), our Creator, for allowing me the great gift of feeling.

I choose to feel everything.

I welcome all the joys and sorrows of loving another human being completely.

I choose to open my heart fearlessly. When it closes, I will endeavor with all of my being to reopen it again and again.

I will act in spite of my discomfort.

I choose relationship commitment.

I will do my inner work to become fit for our relationship.

I choose to love my mate unconditionally, to trust, to forgive, to be kind.

I choose **Soul Freedom**.

The universe and God will support me in doing what I love to do.

In following my bliss, I will act to move forward regardless of how difficult or hopeless my circumstances might seem.

I have faith that in offering to be of service to God, by using my natural talents and abilities in manifesting my vision, I will find a way through challenges, adversities, setbacks, and defeats. Ultimately, I will have the true desires of my heart.

I choose to surrender completely to God's will, knowing that however badly things might seem to be going in the present moment, just around the corner is something better than I could possibly have imagined, planned for, or accomplished with my own willpower.

I choose to be completely and totally free.

When you reclaim and integrate your Four Freedoms, you open wide the gates to the garden of love. Here you reap what you sow—a harvest of abundance, joy, and love that surpasses all understanding.

part 2
FOUR FREEDOMS EXERCISES

Reclaim your Four Freedoms through awareness and action. Manifest the ideas you've just read about by engaging in these exercises. Delight your body, awaken your mind, open your heart, and free your soul. Exercises are organized under the following headings: Body, Mind, Heart, Soul, and Integration. They are further divided into activities for experimenting on your own (marked by one line running down the side of the page) or with your partner (marked by two lines). If you like, you can also do the solo practices at the same time as your partner does them. In addition, some partner exercises can be adapted for individual enjoyment—use your imagination. A note for all exercises: the pronouns *he* and *she* are used interchangeably throughout, meaning that the exercises are for both men and women unless specifically designated for male or female. Cultivate a sense of playfulness, experimentation, and adventure in your practice.

Body Freedom Exercises
TO DO ON YOUR OWN

Fit for Sex

PC pumping—contracting and relaxing the pubococcygeous muscles in your genital area—is your most important exercise for physical sexual fitness. To first feel this muscle group, stop and start the flow when you are urinating.

PC pumping has many benefits for both men and women, including:

- *Preventing or relieving incontinence*
- *Keeping a healthy prostate*
- *Increasing frequency and strength of orgasm for women*
- *Strengthening erection capacity*
- *Delaying ejaculation*

Time for Exercise: four minutes

Properties Required: none

Steps

1. Inhale slowly through your nose.

2. Count to five as you gently hold your breath.

3. Exhale slowly through your nose.

4. Inhale again and slowly tighten your PC muscles.

5. Hold your breath for a count of five as you hold the PC contraction.

6. As you slowly exhale, relax your PC muscles.

7. Repeat twenty-four more times.

8. Endeavor to keep the rest of your body relaxed during your PC contraction.

Comments

You might find that as you contract your PC muscles, other muscles tighten as well, such as your abdomen, shoulders, and buttocks. If you make PC pumping a regular part of your life, you will gradually be able to stay relaxed while you contract specific muscles within the PC group. You can do PC pumping anywhere and anytime, even while you are engaged in other activities, such as driving, talking on the phone, or waiting in line. Build up to one hundred or more PC squeezes per day.

Body Gazing

The commercial media encourage you to see your body as an ongoing renovation project—one that will never be completed and that can never quite conform to the ideal type, no matter what you do. As a result, too many people are unhappy with their bodies, seeing them as too short or tall, too fat or thin, or the wrong color, size, or shape. You might not like your skin, feet, hands, fingers, nose, ears, lips, buttocks, legs, stomach, biceps, breasts, penis, or vagina. You might think there are always parts of your body that need improvement. Seeing yourself this way is not only silly but also tragic, because shame and embarrassment impede surrendering sensually, sexually, and passionately to your lover.

This simple body-gazing exercise can help you recognize the beauty of your natural body just as it is, without any repairs, additions, or subtractions. It will help you know that your body, the temple of your soul, is perfect as it is. It is your gift from the Creator. Instead of trying to make over your body into something else, why not discover what wonderful things you can do with it?

Time for Exercise: five to thirty minutes

Properties Required: full-length and/or hand-held mirror

Steps

Part One

1. Select a part of your body that you are pleased with. For example, you might consider that you have great legs, beautiful eyes, or a lovely mouth.

2. Spend several minutes gazing at that part of your body. Notice the lines, shapes, curves, textures, colors, or other features.

3. Close your eyes and call up the image of that body part in your imagination.

4. Manipulate the image in your imagination, viewing it from different angles, e.g., from above, below, or off to the right or left.

5. Move the image close to your mind's eye, then push it away.

6. See the image in color, then in black and white.

7. Make the image very large and then very small.

8. Notice how each of those changes makes you feel about that body part.

Part Two

1. Select a part of your body that you are critically judgmental about. For example, you might think your belly is too flabby, your hips are too wide, or your thighs are too skinny.

2. Spend several minutes gazing at that part of your body. Notice the lines, shapes, curves, textures, colors, or other features.

3. Close your eyes and call up the image of that body part in your imagination.

4. Manipulate the image in your imagination, viewing it from different angles, e.g., from above, below, or off to the right or left.

5. Move the image close to your mind's eye, and then push it away.

6. See the image in color, then in black and white.

7. Make the image very large and then very small.

8. Notice how each of those changes makes you feel about that body part.

Comments

How you see yourself in your mind's eye affects how you feel about your body. Here are some common possibilities. Feelings are *less intense* when you push the image of your body part far away so it becomes very small, view it as a still shot, see it in black and white, and move the image far off to the edges of your field of vision. Feelings are *more intense* when you bring the image close up so it becomes large, view it as a moving picture, see it in full color, and change your point of view. Experiment with changing the images to learn what diminishes and increases intensity as you visualize your body parts. Once you have learned how this process works for you, use the techniques that diminish intensity when thinking about the body parts you don't like, and use the techniques that increase intensity when thinking about the body parts you do like. Gradually, your negative feelings about particular body parts will diminish.

Tantalizing Tastes

Time for Exercise: fifteen minutes to one hour
Properties Required: cookbook, pen, and paper

Steps

1. Pick a recipe from any cookbook.

2. Add sexy words and images to any part of the recipe to create an erotic poem. (Food and poetry are so deliciously sensual.)

    Here is an example to give you the idea:

    Tomato-Basil Soup Recipe
    Sauté the onion and garlic in olive oil in a skillet until tender. Add the tomatoes. Cook over medium heat for ten minutes. Add the tomato sauce, broth, cream, and half of the basil. Simmer for thirty minutes. Process in a blender until smooth. Return to the pan. Add the bread, remaining basil, and Parmesan cheese. Season with salt and pepper. Garnish with additional cheese, oil, and pesto if desired.

    Tomato-Basil Erotica, or Thirty Minutes Would Never Be Enough!
    Sauté your lover with onions and garlic,
        thrusting heavy on the garlic.
    Rub penis and clit together, drenched in warm olive oil,
        until tender but still firm—
        "al dente," molto bene!
    Sauce it up by spreading overripe tomatoes onto tummies,
        using soft circular strokes
        slowly at first then speeding up,
        sigh and moan to adjust temperature to boiling
        but do *not* allow penis-Vesuvius to erupt!
    Simmer all day and all night, and the next day if desired,
        thirty minutes would never be enough.
    Blend together, golden rod and fig pocket, mortar and pestle,
        keeping everything smooth.
    Turn the heat on and off,
        squeezing the golden rod to add cream
        at the very last moment.

Variation

Read your poem to your lover.

Sensational Scents

Your sense of smell is intricately connected to your brain's memory function and is a source of great erotic pleasure.

Time for Exercise: one or more hours

Properties Required: private vehicle or public transportation

Steps

1. Identify stores that offer a selection of essential oils and others that offer a selection of fine perfumes. Find the locations of the stores you have selected, and map out your travel itinerary around town to visit them.

2. Visit the stores and sniff the sample bottles of essential oils or perfumes to determine your favorites.

3. At home, experiment with adding your selections to your bathing, lovemaking, ritual, and ceremonial practices:

   • Add a few drops of essential oil to your bath water.

   • Place a drop or two onto the vacuum filter.

   • Put a drop or two in an essential oil diffuser (with a tea light or specially designed night light).

   • Experiment with making your own scented massage-oil blends.

   • Add a drop or two to a piece of cotton and place it in a drawer.

   • Lightly perfume between your breasts, around your genitals, anus, feet, and so on (being careful of mucous membranes).

Variation

Take your sensory trip with your lover. Pick scents that turn you both on.

Comments

With essential oils and perfumes, buy the most expensive you can afford. To distill the essence of a fragrance requires a very large quantity of original plant material, hence the high cost for rare quality scents. If your nose is sensitive to smell, the extra cost for the finest fragrances is well worth it.

Health food stores, New Age stores, and many bookstores carry a selection of essential oils. There are also many online retailers. Do a search for essential oils at Google.com and you will easily find a supplier.

Yummy Yoni (For Women)

Women are often taught, subliminally or overtly, that their genitals are smelly, dirty, and ugly. This exercise will help you see the power and the glory in your beautiful yoni *(Sanskrit for "vagina" or "vulva").*

Time for Exercise: ten minutes to one hour
Properties Required: hand mirror

Steps

1. Sit or lie down naked on the bed. You might want to prop pillows behind your back for support.

2. Position the mirror so that you can clearly see your yoni. As you look, appreciate your uniqueness, the elements of your yoni that make you exclusively you. Note the texture of your pubic hair, the size and shape of your outer and inner lips.

3. Find your clitoris and pull back gently on the hood to see your "love button."

4. Spread your lips and look inside your sacred cave. Notice the different colors of your skin.

5. Move past your yoni to view your perineum (the urogenital triangle in front of the anus) and anus.

6. Squeeze and relax your PC muscles. Appreciate the enticing movement your yoni makes!

Variations

• If you are feeling more adventurous, masturbate as you watch in the mirror and watch the changes that your yoni goes through as you become more and more excited. See how your lips and clitoris swell, change color, and become slick with love lubricant.

• Another day, push yourself a little farther and invite your lover to go on this in-depth yoni tour with you. Proudly share your beauty (see "I'll Be Watching You," page 78).

• If you have a digital camera, allow your lover to take pictures of your magnificent yoni at different times during lovemaking so that you can see the beauty of your sexual awakening.

Body Freedom Exercises
TO DO TOGETHER

Sacred Bathing

Time for Exercise: fifteen minutes to one hour

Properties Required: fine bath soaps, bath oils, bath salts, bubble bath, fresh or dried flower petals, shampoos, incense, essential oils, music, candles, refreshments (optional)

Steps

1. Make sure the room is wonderfully warm.

2. Fill the bath with water at a temperature that suits both of you.

3. Add the following to the water as you prefer: bath salts, bath oils, or bath bubbles. Fresh flowers are particularly beautiful floating in the water.

4. Make the rest of the bathroom as lovely as you can by adding candles, houseplants, or fresh flower arrangements to the area.

5. Light incense or heat essential oils in diffusers.

6. Play sexy, sensual, or spiritual music.

7. Bring in a cool, exotic drink or a glass of wine for your refreshment during the bath.

8. Spread something soft on the floor to step onto when you finish the bath.

9. Get into the bath with your lover.

10. When you are finished bathing, dry your bodies with your most luxurious towels.

Variations

• Take turns washing each other's body and hair.

• Shave each other.

• Dry each other.

• Rub some delightful body lotions on each other after the bath.

Comments

If you don't have a bathtub, you can share a shower together. Baths are preferable for sacred bathing, as there is a ceremonial significance to submerging in water. However, even a sponge bath with a bucket will do to cleanse the dirt from your bodies and drop away the cares of the world. Extended Tantric loving times often begin with a sacred bath ritual.

Sweet Feet

Time for Exercise: fifteen minutes to one hour

Properties Required: plastic dishwashing pan, two towels, bar of fine soap, sloughing cream, pedicure items (e.g., pumice stone, toenail clippers, nail file, nail buff, nail sticks, nail polish, foot creams, and lotions)

Steps

1. Gather your items together and fill the pan with hot water. You might also add an essential oil to scent the water (see "Sensational Scents," page 59).

2. Have your barefoot lover sit comfortably in a chair. If he is wearing pants, roll them up above his knees.

3. Sit at his feet. Place one towel on the floor, and set the dishpan on the towel. The other towel is for drying his feet.

4. Place his feet in the hot water to soak. Soak his feet for about five minutes before you begin the pedicure. During the pedicure, make loving eye contact every once in a while to let your lover know you enjoy pampering him.

5. Slough away dead, hard skin with sloughing cream and/or pumice stone.

6. Trim his toenails if required. File the nails for shape.

7. Push back the cuticles with a pedicure nail stick.

8. Buff the nails.

9. Suck on your lover's squeaky-clean toes and drive him into delicious delirium.

10. Apply foot lotion.

11. Apply nail polish (optional, but great fun for him).

Variations

• Take before and after photos.

• Shorten this exercise to just washing the feet and applying foot lotion as a wonderful gift to your lover after a hard day at work.

• Lengthen this exercise by adding a foot massage and/or acupressure treatment to help your lover feel absolutely wonderful.

Baby Body

Safety, security, acceptance, and belonging are universal human needs. The Baby Body exercise offers these things as unconditional gifts of love.

Time for Exercise: five minutes
Properties Required: none

Steps

One of you holds the other with unimaginable tenderness, as if you were holding a trembling infant. Gently rock and caress your lover as you whisper words of comfort, safety, acceptance, and caring.

Comments

This is not intended as a sexual activity. It is very important to offer this as an unconditional gift of love and caring. No performance of any kind is required from the one receiving this gift. Don't let the utter simplicity of this activity fool you; it is immensely powerful and effective. Do this exercise once a week for each other. You can also offer it to your children, your parents, your brothers and sisters, and your friends.

Body Sounds

The body makes very interesting internal sounds, including those of digestion as food moves through the stomach and intestines, the heart beating and pumping blood, breathing, and eating food, including chewing and swallowing. Listen to these sounds, become familiar with them, and notice how they change under certain conditions.

Time for Exercise: five to fifteen minutes

Properties Required: food snacks, water, stethoscope (optional)

Steps

Place your ear on your lover's body at different places.

1. Have your partner lie on her stomach. Place your ear on the small of her back. Move from side to side and up and down her back. You will notice a number of sounds, including digestion, breathing, and heart pumping, depending upon location.

2. Instruct her to roll over onto her back, and place your ear on her belly. Once again, move your ear from side to side and up and down.

3. Have your lover chew some food on the right side of her mouth, and hold your ear against her left cheek.

4. As she swallows, hold your ear at her neck, then her chest, then her stomach to discover what you hear. Try hearing the different sounds made as she chews different kinds of food.

5. Ask her to drink some water. Notice the difference between the sounds of liquid and food being swallowed.

If you can obtain a stethoscope, you can hear many more wondrous sounds from inside the body.

Variations

• Write a short paragraph or poem about the sounds you have heard.

• Heartbeats: notice how the sound changes when she is excited, completely calm, exerting herself physically, and before and after lovemaking.

Comments

This exercise helps you become more intimately familiar, comfortable, and accepting of the human body—yours and your lover's.

Minute Massage

Massage makes your body happy. Its many benefits include stress reduction, lower blood pressure, enhancement of inner security, increased self-worth, relaxation, smooth energy flow within the body, and, of course, pleasure.

You can give a full-body massage in five to seven minutes, but sometimes you will want to linger for an hour or more. You can quickly learn the skills of massage with a little practice. If you feel shy about giving massage, consult the slew of good books and videos available at your local bookstore or library or online. The best way to learn is to give a massage and ask your lover to provide you with lots of feedback so you can adjust motion, pressure, and speed for different parts of the body and for different moods. For example, erotic massage is quite different from relaxing massage, and relaxing massage is different from rejuvenating massage.

Giving a massage on a bed works well if the massage lasts only a few minutes. For longer massages, it is much more comfortable for the masseur to be standing up. Since massage tables are rather expensive, try a mat covered with a sheet on your kitchen or dining-room table.

Time for Exercise: five minutes to two hours

Properties Required: massage oil, mat covered with sheet or light blanket (optional)

Steps (for a five-minute, full-body massage):

1. Be sure the room is warm enough for complete nudity.

2. Start by whispering a few words of endearment into your lover's ear. For example, "This is for you because I love you and want you to know how special and beautiful you are. You are a wonderful man. I love to touch your body. I love to give you pleasure."

3. Begin at his feet and move toward his head with long, firm strokes using your full hand—palms and fingers. Upward strokes revitalize the body. Pace yourself so you can cover the entire body in the time you have allotted.

4. End the massage by whispering a few words of endearment into your lover's other ear. For example: "Thank you for allowing me to touch your beautiful body. Your skin is wonderful to touch. It brings me great pleasure touching you. I love you, my darling."

Comments

Since giving full-body massages need only take a few minutes, you can be generous in offering them to your lover. Give each other short, full-body massages once a week or more frequently.

You don't have to buy expensive massage oils; make your own. You can use any light, fresh cooking oil for the base. Add a few drops of one or several essential oils that you both find pleasing. Don't overdo the essential oils. Essential oils are very strongly concentrated, and at full strength some of them can irritate or even burn sensitive skin, especially around the genitals and eyes. For proportions, we recommend four to eight drops of essential oil per 4 ounces (120 milliliters) of oil.

Here is a recipe for the massage oil supplied in the love kits at Four Freedoms weekend retreats:

4 ounces (120 milliliters) canola oil
4 drops ylang ylang essential oil
1–2 drops black pepper essential oil
1–2 drops clary sage essential oil

Pleasure Points

Acupressure releases muscle tension and eliminates the toxins held in muscle tissue, enabling energy and blood to flow freely. As blood circulation increases, oxygen and other nutrients can nourish more areas of the body, naturally heightening your sensuality. Many of the same points that are therapeutic can also be used erotically. The Pleasure Point practices below are excellent erotic warm-ups for lengthy lovemaking.[1]

Time for Exercise: thirty minutes to one hour

Properties Required: each other

Steps

How to apply pressure to the points:

- Use your fingertips to push straight down on the spot.

- Start softly and very gradually increase the pressure.

- Ask your partner to let you know when the pressure is right.

- Maintain the pressure for a minimum of one full minute (longer on spots your lover particularly enjoys).

- Most important is to focus fully on what you are doing and to send love through your touch.

Pleasure Points for Women

She lies on her back. Work your way slowly and tantalizingly up her body with light, gentle caresses as you move from point to point.

1. Big toes, at the base of the nail, on the outer and inner corners—massage her feet first, then gently press these points.

2. The groin creases, where her thighs join the trunk of her body—put the heels of your palms in these creases and, with your fingertips lightly on her belly, slowly lean your weight forward.

3. Nipples—roll them in your fingers, gradually increasing speed and pressure, and then suck them.

4. Sides of neck—gently nibble and suck on these highly erotic spots.

5. Sacrum (indentations at the base of her spine)—slide your hands under her body and, pressing into these spots with curved fingers, let her weight provide the pressure.

6. Belly, one to two inches below her navel and above the pubic bone—apply gentle pressure here with the palm of one hand as you begin to tickle her clitoris with the fingers of the other.

Pleasure Points for Men

He lies on his back. Use long, firm strokes on his flesh as you move from point to point.

1. Sacrum—straddle him and place your fingertips in the indentations at the base of his spine, allowing his weight to provide the pressure. This triggers nerves that reach into the genitals.

2. Belly—press your fingertips in a downward-pointing straight line starting one to two inches below his navel and ending just above the pubic bone. Breathe in harmony together (see "Harmony Breath," page 143).

3. Pubic bone—place the heels of your hands on the pubic bone, fingertips on his belly, and gradually lean your weight onto him. Encourage him to rock his pelvis as you press.

4. Groin creases, where his thighs join the trunk of his body—put the heels of your palms in these creases and, with your fingertips lightly on his belly, slowly lean your weight forward.

5. Inner thighs—slowly and firmly stroke his inner thighs from about halfway up his thigh all the way to the groin crease.

6. Perineum, between his testicles and anus—with one hand, gently push the tips of your fingers against his perineum at about the halfway point, slightly more toward the anus. With the other hand, lightly stroke his penis.

The Parts Party

Ignorance about human anatomy is monumental. Find out about each other's parts, where they are, what they do, and how they are related to reproduction, sexual function, and sexual pleasure.

Time for Exercise: five to fifteen minutes per session (several sessions highly recommended)

Properties Required: modern atlas of human anatomy, which can be borrowed from your local library, or one of these online resources:

- Free edition of Gray's *Anatomy of the Human Body*: http://www.bartleby.com/107/
- The University of Minnesota maintains an excellent introductory anatomy website, including anatomy quiz tutorials: http://www.gen.umn.edu/faculty_staff/jensen/1135/webanatomy/

Steps

1. Alone or with your partner, review the sexual anatomy for males and females.

2. Identify all of the parts listed by location and function performed in the body.

You can do some of your book exploration alone, but at some point come together to have a conversation about what you have learned. For an interesting challenge, describe each other's parts—men explain female sexual anatomy and women describe male sexual anatomy. Wear your "doctor's hats" and keep your sense of humor.

Male Reproductive System and Sexual Anatomy

penis	glans of the penis
foreskin or prepuce	frenulum
corona	testicles
seminal vesicles	ejaculatory duct
prostate	bulbourethral glands
vas deferens or ductus deferens	erectile tissue: corpus cavernosum (two)
	corpus spongiosum (one)

Related Interest (Male)

parasympathetic nervous system (erection)	sympathetic nervous system (ejaculation)
smooth muscles (ejaculation mastery)	rectum
anus (prostate access and sexual pleasure)	

Female Reproductive System and Sexual Anatomy

ovaries   vulva (external genitals)

uterus   clitoris

cervix   labia majora

vagina   labia minora

Related Interest (Female)

G-spot   ovarian cycle

anus (sexual pleasure)   menstrual cycle

rectum

Urinary System (Male and Female)

kidneys   urethra

bladder   urethral sphincter

ureter

Male Endocrine System (Hormones)

testicles   pituitary gland

scrotum

Female Endocrine System (Hormones)

ovaries   uterus

vagina

Touch Me Like This

Time for Exercise: twenty minutes to several hours

Properties Required: any lubricants or sex toys you may use (optional)

Steps

1. Invite your lover to an erotic demonstration of some ways you would like to be touched sexually.

2. Set a time frame or leave time open-ended and see what develops.

3. Be specific in showing and telling your lover what you want. Experiment with using proper anatomical names for body parts (e.g., vulva, vagina, penis, perineum) as well as exotic Eastern terms (e.g., lingam and yoni, jewel and lotus, jade stalk and cinnabar gate), slang terms (e.g., prick and pussy), and your own playful names (e.g., dashing warrior and juicy peach blossom). Use words that turn you on and are clearly understandable for your partner.

4. In addition to naming the part to be touched, you can also give the process, technique, movement, and so on a name. Use one you have found in a book or video, or make one up, e.g., the "corkscrew" for manually stimulating the penis or "feather touch" for stroking the inside of a woman's thighs.

5. Give specific instructions for direction, speed, and pressure. Examples: clockwise, counterclockwise, circular, up and down, in and out; slow, agonizingly slow, slow with stops, fast, very fast; and light, feather light, almost not touching, firm, forceful, hard.

6. Take turns showing each other how you like to be touched.

Variation

Demonstrate how you prefer to use any lubricants and sex toys you may make use of.

Comments

Be sure you both understand this is a playful activity that has nothing to do with judgment or control. It is about adding variety and stimulating your lover's creativity. Showing your lover how you want to be touched does not mean that you do not like the way you are touched now. This exercise also develops a common vocabulary to help you describe body parts and touch techniques, making it much easier to communicate effectively in a playful, nonthreatening way during lovemaking.

High on Hugs

Time for Exercise: ten seconds to one minute per hug

Properties Required: none

Steps

1. Give your lover different kinds of hugs.

2. Ask your lover to guess each hug's meaning.

   Here are some suggestions for hugs with different qualities and varying degrees and types of intimacy:

"I love you" (for a lover)	woman to woman (friends)
"I love you" (for a family member)	woman to woman (lovers)
"I love you" (for a friend)	opposite sex (friends)
a hug for someone you are sexually active with	opposite sex (lovers)
	"I'm afraid, please hold me"
"I could be interested in sex now"	comfort hug ("Everything will be okay")
"I am really horny"	grief hug ("I'm so sorry for your loss")
"Hello"	celebrate success or winning ("Hooray!")
"Good-bye" (short separation)	"Thank you" (small)
"Good-bye" (long separation)	"Thank you" (major)
man to man (friends)	"This is a reward"
man to man (lovers)	"I miss you"

Invent some of your own hugs with particular meanings.

Comments

Determine which hugs are suitable for which people and circumstances. Hug your lover. Hug other people you feel emotionally close to, for example, children, parents, close friends, and coworkers.

Touch Time

BODY
FREEDOM
EXERCISES
to do
together

Time for Exercise: twenty minutes to several hours

Properties Required: water, oil, or silicone lubricants (optional)

Steps

1. Set aside a special lovemaking time for learning about how you each like to be touched.

2. Decide who will touch and who will be touched.

3. The toucher says, "I am going to touch you in two different ways. Tell me which you prefer, A or B."

4. Begin your exploration using two different touches in various places on and inside your lover's body. Ask her to tell you which of the two touches she prefers.

5. If you find a touch your lover really enjoys, give it a name. Be creative and daring. You will begin to establish a common touch vocabulary for playful and easy communication during lovemaking. Next week you might hear your lover fervently gasp, "Oh darling, please give me the ice cream cone!"

Variations

Take turns giving and receiving the touches.

Comments

With sexual touching, you don't apply the golden rule of "Do unto others as you would have them do unto you." Everyone likes to be touched differently, and you can't possibly know in advance how your lover likes to be caressed. Even highly skilled lovers must learn how to touch each new partner.

This playful technique eliminates the problem of ego sensitivity to perceived criticism. If you think you are being criticized or rejected for the way you are touching your lover, you might experience feelings ranging from mild embarrassment to full-blown shame and varying degrees of low self-esteem. The "touch-me" process eliminates all of the responses that say "No," "Not like that," "I don't like that," "You are doing it wrong," and so on. The feedback you give your lover is always positive, never negative.

Stunning Sensory Stimulation

We rely on our eyes, sometimes at the expense of our other senses, which can become dulled with-
out attention and use. This fun-filled exercise awakens you once again to the mystery of sound,
touch, smell, and taste.

Time for Exercise: thirty minutes

Properties Required: blindfold; items for stimulating these senses: sound, touch, smell, taste. Select nine or more items for each sense. Some suggestions are:

- *Sound*: wind chimes, gong, music box, Velcro strip, crinkly paper, crystal goblet, rattle, whistle, spoons

- *Touch*: warm lotion, powder, bath sponge, feathers, silk, fur, wooden massage roller, cotton balls, ice cubes, pot scrubber, rough fabrics, wool, leather

- *Smell*: dried herbs and spices, body powder, women's perfume, men's aftershave, fish sauce, coffee, cheese, incense, fresh flowers

- *Taste*: fruits, chocolate, candies, nuts, hot sauce, vegetables, liqueurs, breads, cheeses, olives, anchovies

Steps

1. Gather your sound, touch, smell, and taste properties.

2. Sit your lover down and blindfold him.

3. Lean close and whisper playfully into his ear something like, "If you would like to, I'll take you on a wonderful journey through the world of your senses."

4. Begin with the sense of sound. Using your selected items, make each sound for approximately fifteen seconds. Take a fifteen-second break between sounds.

5. After a minute's pause, proceed to the sense of touch. Gently stroke or tickle your lover's skin—face, neck, arms, hands—with the items in your touch toolkit. Go slowly; fifteen seconds per item, with a fifteen-second break between, works well.

6. Move on to smell and finally taste, proceeding as before. When exploring taste, feed dainty bits to your partner with your fingers or daringly pass them mouth-to-mouth.

Comments

Go *very* slowly, so that your partner can respond to each exquisite sensation. Be daring and playful, but also be respectful. If you are the receiver, endeavor simply to experience the sensation, not identify or name it. Do this again another day, switching roles. Use different sense stimulators.

Body Painting

Time for Exercise: thirty minutes to two hours

Properties Required: washable body paints, drop cloth

Steps

1. Place the drop cloth (an old bed sheet or large piece of plastic) on the floor to protect it.

2. Get naked.

3. Take turns painting each other's bodies.

4. Admire each other's beauty.

5. Take turns washing the paint from each other in a bath or shower.

Variation

Take photos of your finished body art.

Comments

You can buy washable, nontoxic paints at children's toy stores and most department stores. Be sure to have a variety of different colors to choose from. You can shower and repaint any number of times.

Dirty Dancing

The phrase "dirty dancing" comes from the movie by the same name, but actually there is nothing dirty about doing a striptease for your lover. This is one of the most erotic gifts you can give each other.

Time for Exercise: fifteen to thirty minutes

Properties Required: music selection(s), sexy clothes

Steps

• Variation one: Take your clothes off, accompanied by some favorite music that turns you on and makes you want to move sensually.

• Variation two: Start naked and put your clothes on while your lover watches. This can be wonderfully erotic. Music is optional. There is a wonderfully sexy "getting dressed" scene in the movie *Don't Look Now,* directed by Nicolas Roeg and starring Julie Christie and Donald Sutherland.[2]

Comments

You don't really need lessons to take clothes off or put them on while your lover watches your sexy moves, but if you are shy and want a few pointers on technique, porn star Nina Hartley and professional exotic dancer Fawnia Mondey have produced a number of excellent instructional videos that help both women *and* men learn how to do hot stripteases.[3]

I'll Be Watching You

Time for Exercise: two minutes to one hour

Properties Required: none

Steps

Ask your lover for permission to watch as she does things that might ordinarily be completely private. Some ideas of things you can ask to observe: undressing, dressing, any particular aspect of dressing or undressing (e.g., putting on stockings), meditating, going to the bathroom, masturbating, self-massage, practicing various forms of exercise or martial arts, and dancing. You might also ask to observe acts of personal hygiene, such as bathing, showering, shaving, caring for fingernails or toenails, brushing teeth, washing hair, or applying perfumed scents and body lotions.

Variations

- Ask permission to perform the act for your lover. For instance, ask to wash his hair or shave her legs.

- The first time you watch, maintain complete silence. If you repeat the exercise and watch again, add sensual, loving comments.

- Watch from outside through a window, pretending your partner is not aware of anyone watching.

Comments

Don't be surprised if your lover cannot grant all of your requests at first, but keep in mind that to experience ecstasy, where the boundaries between the two of you disappear and you merge together as one, you must be able to surrender utterly to your lover. You must become emotionally vulnerable and transparent. This exercise is a playful way to learn to surrender to each other.

Games Galore

Time for Exercise: thirty minutes to all day and night
Properties Required: varies with each game

Treasure Hunt I

Place notes around the house with clues to lead your lover on a search for sensual, sexual treasures. The hidden treasures are treats you will give your partner, such as a full-body massage, a foot bathing, lingam or yoni massage, nude photo session, or fantasy of her choice.

Treasure Hunt II

Leave notes around the house with messages leading your lover from place to place, ending at a spot where you are waiting and ready to make love. If it is nighttime, turn off all of the lights and leave a trail of tea lights to guide your lover to you.

Lipstick Love

Leave red lipstick kisses all over the house: on the new roll of toilet tissue; on the bathroom mirror and other mirrors; on the computer screen; on paper cut-outs taped to walls, counters, and furniture; in his lunch box, briefcase, suitcase, drawers, toolbox, golf bag, bowling-ball bag, or gym workout bag; in the pockets of his clothes; inside his shoes; and so on.

Rent-a-Thrill: Poor Man's Thrill Variation

Hire a cab and make out in the back seat while being driven around.

Rent-a-Thrill: Rich Man's Thrill Variation

Rent a very special and expensive car, such as a Mercedes, Jaguar, Porsche, Corvette, or Hummer. Drive to a secluded location, park, and make love in the car.

Comments

If you use your imagination, you will be able to come up with playful, sensual, and sexy ways to delight each other. Do your planning alone or together, but take turns with responsibility for creating and initiating the next fun game to play together.

Mind Freedom Exercises
TO DO ON YOUR OWN

The Witness

When you act without thinking, caught up in habit, emotional overreaction, or conditioned behavior, you become powerless. Cultivating your observer consciousness—the ability to see yourself objectively as you act and react in your daily life—gives you the power of choice. This simple exercise helps you start to awaken your witness.

Time for Exercise: five minutes

Properties Required: none

Steps

For five minutes today, put on your "witness hat" and observe carefully and in detail what you are doing. For example: "Now I'm walking to the fridge to get an ice cream snack. Why do I want it? Because I'm bored and tired. Is there something else I can do instead? All right, I'll have a long drink of water and then relax with a good book for a few minutes. Now I'm getting a glass and filling it with water. I'm drinking the water, and it feels cool and refreshing. I'm walking slowly toward the bookshelf to select a book . . . (and so on for five minutes)."

Comments

Although you might feel silly, speaking aloud your observations helps you witness. Doing things that make you feel a little foolish helps you move past the tendency to take yourself too seriously. Life is serious, but it doesn't have to be grave.

What I Notice Today

Your relationship is like a garden. You must pay attention to it every day, weeding a little here and watering a little there, so that it will thrive.

Time for Exercise: two minutes

Properties Required: none

MIND
FREEDOM
EXERCISES
to do
on your own

Steps

1. Look closely at your relationship actions. What have you done *today* to support, encourage, or nourish your relationship?

2. If you haven't done anything, come up with a plan of action and follow it through. Your action can be simple or grand. Some suggestions:

   - Give your lover a back rub.

   - Buy your sweetheart a rose.

   - Let your partner relax while you clean up after dinner.

   - Hold hands as you go for a walk.

Flexible Thinking

You have the power over what *you think about. You also have the power over* how *you think about what you think about.*

Your brain performs various functions, such as recalling, thinking, and imagining, in particular ways. Each of your five senses includes a number of subcategories of information—submodalities. When you experience or remember something joyful, painful, or frightening, you do so in a unique way, using particular senses and their submodalities. By consciously changing the submodalities you use to remember experiences, you actually change your memories and assign them different meanings.

MIND
FREEDOM
EXERCISES
*to do
on your own*

Time for Exercise: thirty minutes to one hour

Properties Required: pen and paper

Steps

1. Recall an extraordinary experience in which you felt joyous, happy, and full of wonder. This can be any experience, from any place and any time.

2. Identify your key submodalities for this type of experience and take notes on paper. For example, if you are primarily *visual*, is the picture up close or far away? What color is the background? Is the picture bright or dim? Is the picture black and white or in color? Is the picture moving or still? Is the picture associated (as if you were right in the scene re-experiencing it) or disassociated (as if you were watching a movie)? Where in your consciousness is the picture located, for example, front and center, front lower right, behind your head, high up, or low?

    If you are primarily *auditory*, is the sound loud or soft? Is it slow or fast? Is it continuous or interrupted? Which direction is the sound coming from? Is the sound stereo or monaural? Is it close or far away? Is it rhythmical or discordant? Do you hear music and/or talking? Is the experience associated or disassociated? Is the sound inside or outside you?

    If you are primarily *kinesthetic*, do you notice weight, pressure, temperature, and/or movement? Does your skin feel tactile sensations? Do your muscles and internal organs feel sensations? Where are these located? Do they fade in and out, or are they continuous? How long do they last? Where do they start and end if they move around?

3. Recall any ordinary sexual experience. Don't pick one that was extraordinary (either great or awful). Identify your key submodalities for this experience as you did above—visual, auditory, and kinesthetic details.

4. In your imagination, deliberately change one submodality (visual, auditory, kinesthetic) at a time so that your inner experience for the ordinary sexual encounter is perceived in the same way as the joyous experience. For example, if the ordinary experience is primarily visual with the picture fuzzy, far away, off to one side, fading in and out, and black and white, but the joyous experience is clear, close up, centered in your field of vision, and in color, deliberately change how you see the ordinary experience. Make it clear, close up, centered, colorful, and so on. Notice how this changes your remembrance of the sexual experience and your feelings about it.

Comments

You can use this process to change your perceptions of not just sexual experiences, but any situation.

Best Friends

How well do you really know each other? How much do you take each other for granted?

Time for Exercise: fifteen minutes to one hour

Properties Required: pen and paper

Steps

1. Answer the following questions:

What color(s) are your lover's eyes?

What color is your lover's hair? Is the hair on your lover's body all the same color? Compare the hair on his head, face, arms, legs, chest, pubis, and so on.

How much does your partner weigh?

How tall is he?

What is the name of the perfume or aftershave or other scent your partner usually wears? If you were blindfolded, could you pick out your partner by scent alone?

What is her favorite . . .

food	type of music
color	singer
dessert	band
ice cream	game
perfume	movie
actor	TV show
actress	soft drink
sport	alcoholic drink
flower	book
animal	painter
car	poet

When your lover sleeps, does he lie mostly on his back, right side, or left side?

What identifying marks are on your lover's body—scars, moles, tattoos? Where are they?

What is your lover's birthday?

What are your anniversaries together?

first meeting	engaged
first date	wedding
first sex	birth of children
going steady	

Who is his best friend?

What are your partner's likes and dislikes?

2. List three things your partner likes.

3. List three things your partner does not like.

4. How does your partner communicate what she likes and doesn't like as a lover (words, sounds, looks, body language)?

Variation

Share your answers with your lover.

Mind-Field

Our minds can be drunken monkeys, flitting from one thought to the next. When you are trying to concentrate on something but notice you are drifting off to think about something else, use this technique to learn to stay focused. It will also help your thinking process to become quiet, so that your train of thought slows and focuses. You can stop the world, step outside of time and space, and yet remain fully aware in the now moment.

Time for Exercise: five to fifteen minutes

Properties Required: none

Steps

1. Catch your mind wandering off topic.

2. Stop and name the process. For example: "I just realized that I am thinking about something completely different from what I want to be focusing my attention on."

3. Ask these questions: "How did I get from my original topic to this one? What was the bridge that enabled my thought to jump off track to this completely different topic?"

4. Trace your thoughts backward from the last thought you had before you caught yourself off topic, and follow the thought track back to your original focus of attention. You will notice that one image or idea was like another. Your mind switched onto that other track without your awareness and certainly without your conscious permission.

Meditation Example

I am sitting comfortably, trying to be still in body and mind. I notice that I am thinking about buying a new car. Where did the image of a red convertible come from? I call on my short-term memory and work backward through the thoughts that preceded that image: "It is time to start thinking about getting a new car. I remember the mileage on my car is getting high. I get an image of my car. The horn reminds me of the sound of my horn. I hear a horn honk."

Comments

This simple process will enable you to quickly catch your train of thought whenever it jumps off track. Eventually, your thoughts will stay on track more and more. When they do wander, after you've practiced this technique for a while, you will not need to do the thought backtracking process but will be able to just jump back to where you want to be.

Mind Puzzle

Time for Exercise: fifteen minutes to one hour
Properties Required: none

Steps

1. Ask yourself the following questions. The first question is the most important one. All the others follow from that one. The first question is: "Who are you?" Some common answers might include: your name; your various roles (occupation, parent, child, employer, employee, lover, partner, friend, neighbor); your personality; your beliefs; your values; your accomplishments; your knowledge, skills, and abilities; your possessions; your goals and vision; your body; your thoughts; and your feelings.

2. These next questions can be taken in any order. Pick and choose as you like.

   • What if all of the things mentioned above were taken away from you—one at a time, or all at once? Who would be left? Don't let this question scare you. Just let it play around in your consciousness and see what comes up.

   • Is the "self" something that can be contained within the limits of any or all of your answers and the above categories?

   • Does a body have consciousness, or does consciousness occupy a body? What is consciousness?

   • Does the body have a soul, or does the soul have a body? What is the soul?

   • How can you explain experiences when someone's consciousness travels through space and time separately from his body? What do such experiences suggest about the nature of consciousness?

   • In what sense is your personality only a mask you present to the world? Can you allow yourself to change your mask? Why? When? How? What is the "self" if you change your personality?

   • Is the nature of "self" material, like matter and particles, or nonmaterial, like energy and consciousness? Is the "self" both material and nonmaterial? Can the nonmaterial "self" exist/operate/know independently of and if separated from the material body?

   • What is before birth? What does the "self" come out of? What is after death? What does the "self" return to?

   • We know that bodies die. Can the "self" die with the body?

   • We know that energy and matter cannot be destroyed. Can consciousness be destroyed? Or, like energy and matter, can it just change forms, or move to a different place/level/reality?

- If your existence were neither limited to nor dependent upon the body, how would that change how you live, what you decide to do or not do, how you treat the people you love, and how you treat neighbors or strangers?

- If your existence were neither limited to nor dependent upon the body, how would that change how you think about birth, life, and death?

- Who or what is God? Can you know God as a direct personal experience?

Variation

Talk about your ideas with your lover.

Comments

Enrich yourself by asking these profound questions. Be open to some surprises. Let the mystery enter into your experience.

Shaman Says

The term shaman *might have originated in northern Siberia in a region in central Russia known as Tunguska, purported to be the location of a mystical kingdom referred to as Shamballa.[1] A shaman (sometimes magician, sorcerer, witch doctor, or medicine man) has esoteric knowledge that enables him to utilize life force energies for healing and for controlling the forces of nature. When such a master works in alignment with the good, he or she is considered wise. Almost all cultures around the planet have an ancient history of shamanic myth and practice. In many parts of the world, these practices remain current.*

Time for Exercise: five to fifteen minutes

Properties Required: none

Steps

1. Ask yourself, "How would I be and what would I do in this particular situation if I were a wise shaman?"

2. Relax your ordinary thought process and let images and ideas, intuition and insight, come into your consciousness. Open yourself to guidance from your higher self, from the collective consciousness, and from superconsciousness. Ideas might come to you that aren't based on your previous experience or your regular thought process.

3. Use this technique whenever you are stuck for a solution to a problem, for a way out of difficulty, or for a source of creativity, or use it to trigger an "aha!" epiphany.

Comments

People can act themselves into new ways of thinking. If you can imagine something vividly enough, you can actually make it real. What if you could become wise by imagining that you already are?

Mind Freedom Exercises
TO DO TOGETHER

Poet's Prophecy

Having something to look forward to is one of the supreme motivators in life. Helping your partner to see and believe that good things lie ahead is one of the great gifts you can offer. When lovers expect the best from each other, they are more likely to get it. The Poet's Prophecy lets your love know that you believe in him and that you have faith in his ability to express his beauty and greatness.

Time for Exercise: two minutes

Properties Required: none

Steps

1. Identify something your lover is already dreaming about—something he is passionate about or desires strongly. Or imagine some wonderful outcome that neither of you has ever thought of before.

2. Say to your partner something like this: "As I gaze into the future, I prophesy this will come to pass. . . ." Describe in detail the wonderful circumstances you see unfolding.

Comments

That which you prophesy can be some small delight or something grand. You do not need to be realistic, but the process might have more meaning if the possibility you describe is related to something your lover cares deeply about.

How Do I Love Thee?

Time for Exercise: fifteen minutes to one hour

Properties Required: pen and paper

Steps

1. Each of you makes a list of things loved and appreciated about the other.

2. Take turns reading your lists out loud.

Comments

You can never hear too many times why your partner loves, admires, and adores you. Repeat this exercise monthly to make sure you are both still paying attention.

What Matters to Me Sexually

Time for Exercise: fifteen minutes alone and five minutes with your lover
Properties Required: pen and paper

Steps

1. Take fifteen minutes, or more if needed, to identify what really matters to you in love-making. Identify some things that are essential, some things that you prefer, and some things that you dislike. Be as clear and specific as possible. To make your list, complete the following sentences. You can complete each sentence as many times as you want and also add other likes and dislikes.

I really love it when . . .
I really dislike it when . . .
I really could not be happy without . . .
I really could not be satisfied completely without . . .
I prefer that you would . . .
I prefer that you would not . . .
I would be willing to try . . .
I am not yet ready to try . . .
I am afraid to try . . .
I am excited to try . . .
Something new I would love to explore is . . .
Something I heard about and would like to try is . . .
Something that turns me on a lot is . . .
Something that turns me on a little bit is . . .
Something that really turns me off is . . .
Something that turns me off a little bit is . . .
Something that really embarrasses me is . . .
Something I am really ashamed of is . . .
Something I am shy about is . . .
I like you to touch me like this . . .
I like you to touch me here . . .
I don't like you to touch me like this . . .
I don't like you to touch me here . . .

2. Read your list aloud, slowly, to your lover.

Comments

Do a similar exercise for other important aspects of your relationship, for example, showing affection, sharing household responsibilities, handling money, sharing responsibilities for children, or spending time together.

Two Ways Make New Ways

Time for Exercise: fifteen minutes to two hours

Properties Required: pen and paper

Steps

1. Have a conversation during which you identify points of difference, such as ways of thinking or acting, values, and beliefs. Some of these differences might be minor; others might be causing considerable tension in the relationship.

2. Select one item to work with. If you find the process moves smoothly and quickly, you can tackle additional items now; if not, you can save your list for another time.

3. Tell each other what you appreciate, respect, and admire about the other's differences pertaining to each item.

4. Tell each other what you have learned or can learn from the other's unique approach to various issues.

5. If there is something about your own approach that you can honestly change or modify based upon the positive influence your partner has brought to the table, tell her about it, and thank her for her help in making your life better.

Comments

People often waste much time and effort trying to change their partners into themselves. Although this usually does not work, if it does, boredom can set in pretty quickly. Most of us wish to be appreciated and respected for who and what we are right now. This exercise builds tolerance for differences by finding how they can be complementary rather than disruptive. Repeat this exercise as you identify more differences you wish to honor rather than change.

In our relationship, we have enough respect for each other that we avoid any quick dismissal of the other's point of view, perspective, or opinion. Each of us will stop and consider: "If my partner looks at it that way, is there something I could learn?" In this way, we celebrate rather than fight over our differences, while constantly encouraging our own spiritual growth and development without trying to change the other.

You Go First

The poet Alta once wrote, "Let's stop hurting each other. You go first." Somebody has to go first if things are going to change for the better.

Time for Exercise: fifteen minutes to one hour
Properties Required: none

Steps

1. Identify a contentious issue that repeatedly leads to unfriendly disagreements, disrespectful arguments, or violent fights. Work with only one issue at a time.

2. As objectively as you can, try to come to an agreement on what the nature of the issue is, for example, what happens first (how things get started), then what happens next, such as "I do this, then you do that, then this happens. . . ." Try to do this without blaming, judging, or attacking each other about what usually happens. Try to avoid insisting one or the other is at fault and must change or else. In this step, you are objectively describing the process and not getting caught up in the specifics of your issue.

3. Draw straws to see who will go first. The partner with the short straw leads, offering a change in attitude and, most importantly, a specific behavior change to kick-start the resolution process. *Important*: When you go first, you cannot require any reciprocal change from your partner. *You* are offering a change as a way to initiate a peace process.

Comments

This exercise is designed to get the ball rolling; it is not an attempt to completely resolve the issue immediately. We are assuming there is goodwill between you, that you really do love one another and want the relationship to work. Just getting things moving in a new direction with a new dynamic is often all that is needed to clear the way for a completely satisfactory solution to emerge naturally. The next time you use the process, the other person will go first, or you can draw straws to see who goes first each time.

The Whine Cellar

Do you catch yourself whining and complaining needlessly about what ails you and what you don't like? Do you notice your lover doing the same? Whining and complaining rarely elicit compassion from those around us but rather tend to annoy everyone. Certainly it is necessary to deal with real problems, remove blockages, overcome difficulties, and find solutions, but whining does not help the process. The Whine Cellar technique is a simple, elegant, tactful, and respectful way to get rid of whining every time it rears its annoying head.

Set the stage for using this technique by agreeing to give each other permission to identify when the other is whining and to catch your own whining as much as possible and to stop.

Time for Exercise: one minute

Properties Required: none

Steps

1. When you realize you have been whining, own up to it by naming what you were doing. For example, say to your partner, "I just listened to myself and realized that I have been whining."

2. Banish your whining to the Whine Cellar, never to be heard or seen again. Say to your lover, "I am just going to drop this whole business into the Whine Cellar."

3. If you catch your partner whining, say as tactfully as you can, "It sounds like whining and complaining to me. Can we just drop this into the Whine Cellar?"

Comments

Sometimes the thing you or your lover are complaining about is a very real issue that needs to be addressed. If that is the case, after you have dispensed with whining about it, get down to finding a real solution to a real problem. The Whine Cellar is not intended to be an escape from the responsibility you have to become fit for your relationship and to deal honestly with real problems. There is an important difference between problem solving and whining about problems. Both of you will know the difference when you hear it.

Truth and Dare

All the secrets you hold inside are an enormous weight, a needless burden. This exercise offers an excellent opportunity for you to revisit and let go of things from your past that still bother you. All of us have experiences that have left us wounded: times when we felt humiliated, diminished, attacked, violated, abused, rejected, ignored, or misunderstood. Just to have someone listen to your story without judgment, without comment, and without assuming responsibility can lighten your load tremendously.

Time for Exercise: ten to thirty minutes

Properties Required: none

Steps

Share with your partner something you have been thinking or worrying about, are afraid or ashamed of, or embarrassed or otherwise bothered by.

Variations

• Only one person tells his or her story each time you do the exercise.

• Both tell a story during the same session.

Comments

When you share your story, you are not necessarily asking for help or expecting your lover to provide a solution, although you might want these things. If you do, include that information as a request to your lover.

I Changed My Mind . . .

"And she never gives out, and she never gives in. She just changes her mind."
Billy Joel, "She's Always a Woman"

Time for Exercise: ten to thirty minutes
Properties Required: none

Steps

1. Individually select an issue that has been a bone of contention between you and your lover.

2. Offer a new position on that issue than the one you have held onto in past discussions, debates, or arguments. This works best if both of you create a new position, although not necessarily on the same issue. If only one of you moves to a new stance on something, it can feel too much like giving in or giving up.

Comments

There is something about giving in or giving up that connotes defeat. When you give in or give up, often you lose. No one wants to be a loser. But the connotation of changing your mind is completely different. Someone who is incapable of changing is also incapable of growing. Never changing your mind is to be stuck in the past, inflexible, unreasonable, and hard. Changing your mind about things is not only desirable but essential if you are to continue to expand your consciousness, to access more life choices, and to be truly free.

Of course, there is a time to stand your ground, but there is also a time to move to a new position. This exercise helps you begin to discern the difference between when it is appropriate to hold a position firmly, because it represents being true to yourself and your core values, and when it is appropriate to change your position, for example, when you are just insisting you are right only to win an argument or to be in control.

MIND
FREEDOM
EXERCISES
*to do
together*

Completely Committed

Time for Exercise: fifteen minutes

Properties Required: none

Steps

1. Explain to your partner what your commitment means.

2. Give evidence that supports your statement and shows your commitment. Below are examples of evidence that commitment is real. The items on this list are not all required. They are examples to help get the exercise going. Each couple will express its commitment in its own way. There are no rules about commitment. The most important thing about commitment is that you are in agreement about it. For example, in some relationships, neither partner is ready for 100 percent commitment.

   Merging of finances
   Names on property titles
   Shared bank accounts
   Beneficiaries in wills and insurance policies
   Legal marriage
   Having or adopting children
   Sleeping together
   Fidelity
   Personal sacrifices on the other's behalf
   Giving up something you want so your lover can have what he wants
   Admitting when you are wrong rather than always trying to win every argument
   Asking, "How can I help?"
   Offering, "Let me do that for you."
   Confiding in your lover when you are hurting or afraid
   Admitting, "I don't know."
   Asking for what you want
   Saying yes whenever you can, and saying no when you must
   Trying new things together
   Surviving hardship
   Trust—for example, when the evidence makes your partner look bad, you think, "That can't be all the evidence."
   Not putting up with your partner's bullshit, but calling her on it (in a loving way)
   Forgiving your lover when he has made a mistake
   Treating him with kindness, respect, and fairness

Comments

If you have issues about commitment, share them with your lover. Explain any fears and doubts you have about your willingness or ability to give your commitment. Also talk about your intention to work through these issues together.

Posting Priorities

Time for Exercise: five to fifteen minutes

Properties Required: pen and paper

Steps

1. One partner reads the following story to the other.

An expert in time management, who spent a lot of his time in the country-side, came to town on occasion and spoke to business people. Now he stood in front of a group of high-powered overachievers and talked about priorities, stress, relaxation, and time for about an hour and a half. At the end of his presentation, he answered questions and began to think that things had gone well, that his ideas were well received and accepted. Soon, though, someone shouted out that he had spent too much time with the birds and bears and was out of touch. When he asked what the questioner meant, a haggard-looking man answered that his own day filled so quickly with so many things to do—all of them important—that he didn't have time for theories, not even one that promised more time.

"If you remember," the expert answered, "I spoke about inner and outer clocks, about how the mind runs away to convince us everything is important. If you weren't in such an 'inner hurry,' you would have dwelled on that part of my talk a bit more. I specifically pointed out that 'there is no more time'—each day has only twenty-four hours. There's only our capacity to properly use what little time there is."

He then walked to a small wheeled and cloth-covered table and brought it to the front of the stage. He reached under it and pulled out a one-gallon wide-mouth jar and set it on the table in front of him. Then he produced about a dozen fist-sized rocks and carefully placed them, one at a time, into the jar. When the jar was filled to the top and no more rocks could fit inside, he asked, "Is this jar full?"

Everyone in the audience shouted, "Yes."

The conference speaker said, "Really?" as he reached under the table and pulled out a bucket of gravel. He dumped gravel in the jar and shook it, causing pieces of gravel to work themselves down into the spaces between the big rocks. Then he asked the group again, "Is the jar full?" By this time the group was on to him, and the haggard-looking man stayed silent. "Probably not!" someone finally said.

"Good!" he replied, and reached under the table again, bringing out a bag of sand. He dumped the sand into the jar, shaking it so that it fell into all of the spaces left between the rocks and the gravel.

Once more he asked, "Is this jar full?"

"No!" everybody shouted. Once again he said, "Good." Then he grabbed a pitcher of water and began to pour it in until the jar was filled to the brim. Then he looked at the questioner and asked, "What is the point of my illustration?"

The man answered, "The point is, no matter how full your schedule is, if you try really hard, you can always fit some more things in it!"

"No!" the expert replied. "That was not my point. The truth that I demonstrated is: If you don't put the big rocks in first, you'll never get them in at all."

The expert finished off by saying, "Your days are numbered, and your life is like that jar—limited. Every day will always be filled and can only hold so much. But if you put the big rocks in first, you'll be amazed at how much room there really is. Having priorities doesn't mean choosing among many things—it means choosing the important things." And then he added, "Please forgive me for being dramatic. I knew I'd only be with you a very short time and came prepared to show you how time must be managed. Thanks for your attention." And he walked off to great applause.[2]

2. Both of you make a list of the top ten priorities in your life.

3. Compare your lists and discuss the issues this exercise raises in your relationship.

MIND
FREEDOM
EXERCISES
to do
together

Delectable Deliberations

One of the sexiest turn-ons for men and women alike is the intellectual stimulation of exploring and disagreeing about ideas.

Time for Exercise: the length of a meal
Properties Required: none

Steps

1. One of you selects a topic of conversation for a special evening meal.

2. Announce the topic to your partner. *Note:* You can take turns selecting topics.

3. You both do a little research about the topic. If you are able to access the Internet, do a search on Google.com and you will quickly find more information than you have time to digest on almost any topic imaginable.

4. At dinner, instead of silence or mundane discussions about the weather, engage in a lively exchange about the chosen topic.

Comments

Mealtimes can be most stimulating if you go to a little trouble and prepare yourself. Make the times matter by how much you put into this exercise, and you will be richly rewarded.

Fantasy Fun

Fantasies provide opportunities to explore all aspects of sexuality with a lover you trust in a situation that is safe, even though some fantasies might involve danger, violence, or taboos. Suggested guidelines for exploring fantasy:

- *No one gets hurt—no means no, and stop means stop.*
- *Discuss your fantasy in advance and agree to terms and limits.*
- *Use fantasies that bring you closer together and into the moment—don't use fantasies that threaten your relationship or take you away from the here and now.*

Time for Exercise: a few minutes or all day and night

Properties Required: varies with the fantasy

Masks and Costumes

Greet your lover at the door in various costumes: bathrobe with nothing underneath; a mask; bra, panties, garter belt, stockings, and high heels; birthday suit; a tie only; top only; bottoms only; just your socks; thong; war paint on face; body paint with no clothes; or chocolate and whipped cream in special places, no clothes.

Role Plays and Situational Fantasies

Suggested Characterizations: cheerleader, prostitute, dominatrix, airline steward, doctor, nurse, golf pro, dance instructor, fitness trainer, kidnapper

Suggested Role Plays

1. Seduction of delivery person, salesperson, milkman, service person, census taker, meter reader, or any stranger coming to your door.

2. Dress up as the same sex and stage a chance meeting for lovemaking.

3. Employees' clandestine sexual encounter in the photocopy room, bathroom, closet, and so on.

4. Shopping in a store at closing, you are the last ones in the store, and the storeowner locks the door.

5. Shopping in a clothing store, you are trying on lingerie in the fitting room. The light goes off, and a stranger enters the room with you.

6. While attending an interview, you seduce the person interviewing you.

7. A waiter or waitress invites you into the back room for a quickie.

8. You are eating in a restaurant, and you pass a note inviting the waiter or waitress to join you in your car for a quickie.

9. You are at a dinner party, and a stranger seated next to you begins to touch you under the table.

10. You are teenagers making out in the theater balcony.

11. Get into your car (parked in your driveway) and make love as if you were at a drive-in movie.

12. You stop at a red light at a busy intersection. You make eye contact with the person driving the car stopped next to you in the other lane. She follows you for a short distance and motions for you to pull over. She gets into your car, and you have a wild sexual encounter.

13. You have experimented with some drug and have lost all of your inhibitions. You are willing to do anything with your lover.

14. You are detained overnight in the local jail, and you seduce your cellmate.

15. You are abducted and ravished by an alien space invader.

16. You are acting in a stage play or movie. During the rehearsal, performance, or filming of a love scene, you really make love, even though you were expected only to pretend.

17. You are participating in a sexuality research project. You make love while someone watches through a one-way mirror.

18. You are out with your lover at a swingers' club. The easy nudity and open sexuality, including intercourse, turn you on. You slip under the table and make love. You surprise each other, because you have never imagined behaving like this.

19. You are buying fresh produce at the local supermarket. You ask if they have any fresh arugula, and the produce man invites you into the back to pick out what you want. You unzip his pants and pick out more than arugula.

20. Meeting a stranger while swimming in the community pool or at a public beach, you make love in the water.

Comments

In addition to stimulating your creative consciousness, sexual fantasy also encourages you both to become emotionally vulnerable and transparent. By revealing your fantasy, you risk disapproval, judgment, or rejection but win out over anxiety.

For more sexy fantasy ideas, check out these books by Laura Corn: *101 Nights of Grrreat Sex* and *101 Nights of Grrreat Romance.*

Heart Freedom Exercises

TO DO ON YOUR OWN

Flower Power

Painful life experiences can lead you to close your heart like a tender flower that closes its petals against the chill of the night. In this exercise, you learn to consciously open your heart so that you and all around you can share in the heavenly fragrance of its blossom.

Time for Exercise: five minutes

Properties Required: none

Steps

1. Sit quietly, feet flat on the floor, back straight, shoulders relaxed.

2. Close your eyes and breathe slowly and deeply.

3. Focus your attention on your feet and their connection to the ground. They are your roots, anchoring you firmly and safely to the earth.

4. Continue to breathe slowly for a minute as you strengthen and deepen your connection to the earth (see "Grounding," page 132).

5. When you feel well anchored, bring your attention also to your heart energy center. It is in the center of your chest, between your nipples, roughly on a level with your armpits.

6. In your heart center, picture a flower bud.

7. Keeping part of your focus on your connection to the earth, slowly open the flower bud until it is in full bloom.

8. When the bloom is wide open, employ your breathing rhythm to bring loving energy into and out of your heart center. On the inhale, allow loving energy from the universe to flow into your flowering heart center from all directions (front, back, both sides). On the exhale, allow your loving energy to flow out into the universe in all directions.

9. To complete the exercise, slowly come back to the world by shifting your attention from the opened heart blossom to focus only on your roots in the earth.

10. Next, focus only on your breathing rhythm, the gentle inhale and exhale.

11. Notice what is happening throughout your body. Notice your emotional state. Notice your mental state.

12. Open your eyes and continue your day.

Novocain

How do you dull your emotional pain? How do you hide from hurting?

Time for Exercise: five to fifteen minutes
Properties Required: none

Steps

1. Identify any strategies you use to dull, deny, avoid, or suppress emotional pain. The first step for healing emotional pain is to allow yourself to feel it. Once you have identified what the pain is and where it comes from, you can take action to heal it at its source. Common pain-avoidance strategies include: improper/excessive/addictive use of drugs; other kinds of addictive behavior (e.g., with food, sex, power, and violence); obsession with control; wild outbursts of anger, disproportional to the events or circumstances that triggered the anger; excessive talking; avoiding socializing with family, friends, and neighbors; quick judgments about the inadequacy, incompetence, and insensitivity of others; excessive shyness; avoiding all emotional discomfort; seeking pleasure above all else as the only important aspect of life; rigid inflexibility on issues for which there are different points of view; trying to win at any cost; never admitting you are wrong; never admitting you made a mistake; never admitting when you don't know; and never allowing yourself to cry.

2. Identify your pain-avoidance strategies, including when and how you use them and what you use them for.

3. Once you have identified your pain-avoidance strategies, the next time you are tempted to use them, stop yourself and make a conscious decision to allow yourself to admit that you are hurting, afraid, or in pain. Allow yourself to feel these sensations fully.

4. Look to the trigger, source, or cause of the pain and ask yourself these questions:

   How can I heal the cause of this pain?
   Is there any change in behavior that is required on my part?
   Is there some apology I need to make to someone?
   Is there something I need to ask for from somebody?
   Is there some way I can relinquish my attempts to control the situation?
   Is there someone I need to forgive?
   Do I need to forgive myself for something?
   Do I need to allow myself to cry?
   Do I need to talk to someone?
   Do I need to seek some form of therapy?

Do I need to record my struggle in a personal growth journal?

Are there changes I need to make in my life?

5. Expand on answers to the last question above by considering specific areas of life: where you work, where you live, whom you live with, whom you socialize with, how you spend your free time, and how you take care of yourself (eating, sleeping, drugs, alcohol, hygiene, bad habits, watching television, exercise, meditation, prayer, memberships, volunteering, helping others, handling money, saying no).

Comments

Although pain and hurt are unavoidable for anyone who is really alive, suffering is unnecessary and avoidable. The cause of suffering is the failure to deal with the cause of pain. Suffering only exists in the absence of healing.

We encourage you to allow yourself to feel everything—not only the good feelings but the bad ones as well. The way to deal effectively with bad feelings and negative emotions is to heal the cause. It is neither helpful to suppress or cover up your hurting nor to pretend you are well when you are really in pain. Denial of pain only increases your suffering.

Wishes of the Heart

Open your heart. Keep your heart open. Open it again every time it closes.

Time for Exercise: one minute

Properties Required: none

Steps

Imagine the one best thing that could happen for the following people in your life. What if you could grant each of these people one wish? What would it be?

partner or lover	your creditor
each of your children	your landlord
your mom	your teacher
your dad	your guru
each of your grandparents	your best friend
each of your brothers and sisters	a friend who has betrayed you
your next-door neighbors	your mentor
your archenemy	your therapist
your boss or employer	

In a private ceremony, send the wishes of your heart out into the universe so that each of them might be fulfilled.

Comments

It is also important but challenging to send out good wishes of your heart for people you don't like.

Freeing the Fool

Time for Exercise: five to fifteen minutes

Properties Required: none

Steps

When have you felt foolish, embarrassed, or humiliated? Recall the circumstances of those situations. What if these things had happened to someone you love instead of yourself? Would they seem as emotionally loaded and devastating as they were when they happened to you?

The King's Fool

Imagine that you lived at a time when there were kings and that you assumed the role of the king's fool. What is the role of a professional fool? What is the emotional significance of foolish, outrageous, and silly behaviors when they are done consciously?

Do we have to assume that the fool has a negative status? Must the fool be stupid, ignorant, or lacking in intelligence? Is it possible to see the fool as entertainer, as therapist, as possessing properties of kindness, generosity, and wisdom? Is it possible to see the fool as creative, funny, fun, and spontaneous? Can the fool be mature, intelligent, even enlightened? Can the fool be a kind of sorcerer or magician? Can the fool be in humble service to the good? Can the fool be a healer? Can the fool be a most trusted advisor?

Would allowing the fool within you to manifest some or all of these positive qualities improve your life? What are some ways you can allow yourself to lighten up, to act a bit foolish, to stop taking yourself so seriously, and to let go of control?

Try deliberately doing one foolish thing per week for the next four weeks. If you like how those experiments change your life, try acting foolishly once per day.

Comments

The Fool in tarot is a fully realized, self-actualized, splendid human being. He possesses all of the following qualities:

wisdom	self-love/high self-esteem
freedom	self-confidence
courage	loved by children
likable and lovable	trusting
approachable	humble
flexible	risk-taking
creative	independent
fun and funny	cares not what others think of him
heart open	entertaining

accepting/nonjudgmental
lightness of being
open to change
acts in spite of fear
follows his bliss
of service to the good
sharing

feels everything
vulnerable
bridge between heaven and earth
optimistic
comfortable with mystery
surrenders

Heart in Darkness

Time for Exercise: fifteen minutes to one hour

Properties Required: drawing paper, pencils, colored pencils, pen, charcoal sticks

Steps

1. Draw a picture illustrating the emotional state of your heart right now. Convey the extent to which your heart is wounded, healed, open, closed, stingy, generous, and capable of giving and receiving love. For example, your heart might be entombed in an impregnable fortress, or there might be cracks or openings giving some access to your heart. It could be shrouded in darkness or bathed in light. Various colors might symbolize your heart's condition. There might be sores or tears in your heart. It might be impaled with sharp objects.

2. As you undertake an emotional healing journey, a process of awakening your spirit, a quest for freedom, or a deepening of your commitment to your relationship, redraw your heart picture about once per month as a visual representation of your progress.

Variation

Share your drawings with your lover.

Comments

As we heal and become whole, we can often forget how much progress we have made, how much better we feel, and how much the quality of our lives has improved. This is one way to keep a record—a visual journal.

Heart Freedom Exercises
TO DO TOGETHER

Eye Gazing

So through the eyes love attains the heart:
For the eyes are the scouts of the heart,
And the eyes go reconnoitering
For what it would please the heart to possess.

Guiraut de Borneilh

Hours, days, or even weeks might pass by without couples really looking at one another. The brief but powerful practice of conscious eye gazing forges unequivocal bonds. Eyes are gateways for love. Through real and true eye contact, you share your soul.

Time for Exercise: two minutes

Properties Required: none

Steps

1. Sit or stand facing each other.

2. Decide who will send love first.

3. Relax your face. Let your eyes be soft.

4. The first sender allows all of his love to pour out through his eyes into his partner's.

5. She receives it, opening her heart to welcome his love.

6. No words are spoken. There is no movement of arms or hands or body, just the flow of love for one full, rich minute.

7. Switch roles.

8. For one minute, the second sender allows her love to pour out through her eyes into her partner's.

9. He opens his heart to receive her love.

Comments

This is not a staring contest. Looking deeply into each other's eyes is very powerful. You might feel uncomfortable or vulnerable. You might laugh from nervousness or fear. However, if you can bare yourself and share your love in this simple but profound way, your heart will open. You might even shed tears of joy.

HEART
FREEDOM
EXERCISES
to do together

116

Three Out of Three

"I want you. I need you. I love you." Could there be any sentences sweeter than these to hear your lover speak?

Time for Exercise: fifteen minutes
Properties Required: none

Steps

1. Prepare in advance what you will say to your lover for each of these three statements of endearment. What words will accurately and honestly express how much you care for, desire, love, and need your partner? Give some specific examples for each statement.

2. Sit your lover down and gaze into his eyes as you tell him how and why you want, need, and love him.

Comments

Just saying "I want you, I need you, I love you" is far less powerful and moving than if you tell him why and how. For example:

I want you. "You turn me on like crazy. I think about you all of the time. I can't wait to get home from work to touch and smell and kiss you. Holding you in my arms is being in heaven. I want to grow old with you. I want to spend the rest of my life with you."

I need you. "When you are with me, I feel invincible, as if I can handle anything the world throws my way. If you left, my heart would crack, and I would fill buckets with tears. I like myself most when I am with you. You bring out the best and most beautiful in me. Together we can do anything we set our minds to. You are my best friend."

I love you. "When I look into your eyes, little stars fly out into me. Your smile lights up the darkness. Your touch removes all of my fears and doubts. When we make love, it is as if there is only one of us. When we make love, we join hands with God."

Permission, Please

Time for Exercise: one minute

Properties Required: none

Steps

Ask your partner's permission to be her lover. Look into her eyes and hold her hand while you speak. Most important is *how* you speak, not the exact words you use. Put your love into your voice.

Here is an example, but use your own words from your heart:

> "My darling, we have some hours now when we can be together. I want to show you how much I adore you, how much I love you, and how much I desire you. I would love to touch your beautiful body with gentleness as well as fierceness. I want to smell your scent in all your secret places. I wish to taste your fruits of delight. I wish to give you the greatest pleasure. I want to love you in a way that is sacred and full of wonder. May I be your lover?"

Comments

Simple respect is often missing even in the best relationships. By asking permission to make love with your partner, you are showing that you do not take her for granted and how much you respect her. It is wonderfully romantic. Not only men should ask their ladies for permission; men respond well to the same courtesy.

Yin/Yang Yes!

The familiar black-and-white Chinese yin/yang symbol suggests a balance and harmony between the yin (feminine energies) and yang (masculine energies), or between any pair of opposites. Examples of yin/yang in relationship are following/leading, surrender/control, opening to the mystery/making precise plans, and creativity in the moment/habit.

An important issue in many relationships is who leads, who makes decisions, and who is in charge. Sorting out "who's the boss?" can be quite contentious but does not need to be. Many couples are able to switch the lead back and forth depending on the situation and the respective abilities of the partners. They find the complementarities between their differences rather than competitiveness for power and control.

Time for Exercise: two to four minutes per dance

Properties Required: stereo and selection of slow dance tunes

Steps

1. Pick out several of your favorite slow and romantic songs to dance to.

2. During the dance, switch the lead back and forth between you.

3. Switch the lead when a new song comes on or at any time during a tune.

Comments

Yin/yang dancing is a simple, playful way to practice the art of surrender—a core ability in every spiritual practice.

Lovers' Days

Asking your lover for what you want and giving your lover whatever has been requested are two sides of the same coin—a yin/yang balance of receiving/giving and passive/active pleasure. Just as it is important to learn to freely ask for what pleases you, it is also important to know that you can give unconditionally. This playful practice helps you do just that.

Time for Exercise: two afternoons, evenings, or full days
Properties Required: varies with the play

Steps

1. Each partner writes down a description of an ideal day with the other, describing a sensuous day of attention and focus on the writer. Your requests may be sensual, explicitly sexual (see "Touch Me Like This," page 72), gently affectionate, or caring and attentive actions—anything and everything from cuddling and back rubs to storytelling and poetry reading to hours of kissing and exotic intercourse.

2. Decide who is first to receive the attention—draw straws, flip a coin, pick a number. Next time it's the other partner's turn to receive.

3. During your loving time, try to give your partner as many things on the list as you can. Points for you both to remember:

   • You know how to give your lover whatever has been requested without wondering, "What's in it for me?"

   • You know how to give joyously and freely.

   • You know how to receive graciously and respectfully.

   • You deserve to be treated like the king or queen you are.

HEART
FREEDOM
EXERCISES
*to do
together*

Lovers' Scissors

Although this is an intercourse position, in this instance the focus is not on orgasmic release or simple physical pleasure. By combining mental focus, conscious breath, genital connection, and loving eye contact, the Lovers' Scissors brings your masculine and feminine energies into harmony. It opens your hearts, connecting you deeply to your partner.

Time Required: five to thirty minutes, depending on how much time you have

Properties Required: none

Steps

1. Lie perpendicular to each other—heads apart, groins close together. The woman is on her back, the man on his side. To make the scissors, the woman puts the leg that is closest to her partner over the top of his hip. Her other leg she puts between his legs.

2. In this position, the man gently slides his penis into her vagina.

3. Look into each other's eyes (see "Eye Gazing," page 116) and breathe slowly and deeply together (see "Harmony Breath," page 143).

4. Place your hands on each other's hearts.

5. Be quiet and still.

6. Feel your connection through your genitals, through your hands to hearts, through your eyes, and through your breath.

7. Focus your mind on your loving connection. If thoughts intrude, let them pass through and draw your attention back to your genitals, your heart, your eyes, and your breath.

8. To complete your practice, slowly disengage and then give each other a full-body hug.

Comments

This is a great position for ending lovemaking or during lovemaking when you want to catch your breath. Try it as a meditation for starting or ending your day together. Its energetic effects are cumulative—a deeper bond and more patience with each other.

HEART
FREEDOM
EXERCISES
*to do
together*

Love Poems

Time for Exercise: five minutes to one hour
Properties Required: books of poetry

Steps

1. Browse through books of poetry to locate poems that elicit an emotional reaction when you read them. The poems might be about love, romance, commitment, or sex.

2. Copy those you like the most so you have a collection to choose from when you want to read aloud to your lover.

3. Practice reading some of the poems out loud while you are alone.

4. Buy a selection of sensual, erotic love cards. Choose cards with a photograph or drawing but no words inside so that you have room to write your own words in the card.

5. Write your own poem—by far the best, because it comes from your heart—or pick one from the collection you have gathered and copy it into the card. Present the card to your lover at a particularly romantic moment and read the poem aloud.

6. Don't save this activity for only special occasions such as birthdays and anniversaries. This can be a regular part of your extended lovemaking sessions.

Comments

Writing your own poems is something you can learn to do. Using the words of published poets at first will prime your own creativity.

HEART
FREEDOM
EXERCISES
to do
together

Song of Love

Songs of romance are sure-fire heart melters, especially when they are sung just for you by the one you love.

Time for Exercise: three to five minutes to sing

Properties Required: the lyrics to a love song, obtained by listening to a CD, reading inside a CD cover, or searching the Internet

Steps

1. Sit your lover down and sing that song to her.

2. Sing without musical accompaniment. Sing from your heart.

Comments

You might feel shy and uncertain about your voice. Although you might feel vulnerable and even foolish, romance requires trust and daring. Sing your love out loud. Practice beforehand if you like. It is especially endearing and empowering when someone who feels he can't sing at all takes his courage in hand and croons out his love anyway.

Love Potion

The use of sexual stimulants such as alcohol or herbal aphrodisiacs is well established in ancient sacred sex practices such as Tantra. Making your own love potions together is very sensual. Consuming them as part of your lovemaking rituals is even sexier.

More is not better—moderation is best. Consult your physician before consuming any aphrodisiacs.

Time for Exercise: ten minutes to mix up a punch drink

Properties Required: selection of aphrodisiac tinctures, ingredients for punch, canning jar with lid

How to make an aphrodisiac tincture:

- Infuse (soak) the leaves, roots, and/or bark material of a plant (e.g., damiana) in alcohol (e.g., grain alcohol or vodka) for five days. Use 2 cups alcohol (about ½ liter) to ½ ounce or more (about 15 grams) plant material. Store in a closed container to prevent evaporation.

- Strain through a filter, such as a paper coffee filter. Retain the liquid as well as the material in the filter.

- Infuse the plant material from the filter in water for another five days. Use the same amount of water as you did alcohol.

- Strain the liquid through a filter. Combine the two liquids and add a sweetener, like honey, to taste.

Steps

1. Prepare your selection of one or more aphrodisiac tinctures, or buy one already made. They are readily available over the counter at most health food stores.

2. Consume 1 to 2 ounces (about 30 to 60 milliliters) of your homemade brew approximately thirty minutes before lovemaking.

3. If you are using a commercially prepared tincture, three to six drops instilled directly under the tongue brings interesting results.

4. Experiment by adding aphrodisiacs to your favorite punch recipe.

Comments

Here are some suggestions for your aphrodisiac tinctures:

Damiana

"Chemically this plant has been found to contain several alkaloids that directly stimulate the sex organs. . . . Native Mexican women have long drunk an infusion of the herb a couple of hours before retiring to prime themselves for their men. It is reputed to induce erotic dreams when drunk at bedtime."[1]

Yohimbe

"One of the most popular aphrodisiac herbs available, yohimbe has a reputation for producing electrifying sexual encounters. . . . Its notoriety as a potent aphrodisiac, though, probably stems from its use in African orgiastic rituals that sometimes last for two weeks. . . . Some users also report mild hallucinogenic and heightened sensory effects much like those experienced on LSD or MDA."[2]

Muira Puma

Muira Puma has a long history in Amazonia as an aphrodisiac.

A guide to aphrodisiacs is also available on Four Freedoms website: www.tantra-sex .com/aphrodisiacs.html.

I'm Yours

Time for Exercise: fifteen minutes to one hour

Properties Required: colored pens with washable ink suitable for writing on skin

Steps

1. Take turns writing loving, sexy statements on your body and your lover's body.

2. Read each other aloud "like a book."

3. Here are some typical statements to inspire your own expressions: your playground; feel this; your name goes here; help yourself; suck here; look closely; try some; this is yours; apply lotion here; I give this to you; put your face here.

Variation

When your lover's body is sufficiently covered, take digital photos so you will have a record.

HEART
FREEDOM
EXERCISES
*to do
together*

126

We Belong Together (For Men)

Time for Exercise: one hour

Properties Required: length of 1-inch dowel rod or handle, glue, materials for decoration

Steps

1. Buy a 3- to 4-foot (1- to 1.25-meter) length of dowel rod that is 1 inch (2.5 centimeters) in diameter, or cut a section from the handle of an old implement.

2. Gather together the glue and tidbits of colored string and construction paper, earrings, jewelry, painted trinkets, small children's toys, money (coins and bills), small figurines of people, animals or caricatures, and so on, and use the materials you have gathered to decorate the dowel rod.

3. Offer it as a symbol of the commitment of your lingam (Sanskrit for "penis") to your lover.

4. Stand it in a corner or hang it from the ceiling of your bedroom.

5. Swear an oath to your lover that if you decide to have sex outside your relationship, you will take the sacred lingam down. Keeping the sacred lingam in place symbolizes your sexual commitment to your lover—a gift freely and willingly offered in the name of love.

Gift Wrapped (For Women)

Time for Exercise: one to two hours
Properties Required: clay and paints

Steps

1. With clay, papier mâché, or simple Play-Doh, form a likeness of your yoni (Sanskrit for "vagina").

2. Paint your yoni with stunning colors and symbols.

3. Wrap it beautifully.

4. During one of your sacred loving times, present it to your lover as an expression of your love and commitment.

5. Place it on top of a shelf or dresser in your bedroom.

6. Swear an oath to your lover that if you ever decide to pursue sex outside your relationship, you will remove the sacred yoni from its display in your bedroom.

7. Show your man how much you love him by taking his real lingam into your real yoni, gift-wrapping it in your desire.

No Boundaries

Sacred lovemaking has no goal (you are not trying to get to orgasm), but there is a purpose—the union of the lovers. During sexual and spiritual ecstasy, the boundaries between lovers disappear. If you have secrets and barriers to protect yourself emotionally from your lover, you are blocking yourself from experiencing ecstatic union.

Time for Exercise: fifteen minutes to one hour

Properties Required: none

Steps

1. Consciously identify the secrets you keep and the emotional barriers you have erected.

2. Make a list of these, including even your most guarded secrets, and put names (or descriptions) to the barriers you have entrenched around your heart. This might take days or weeks, not just a few minutes of casual thought, because these barriers must be uncovered and brought into your consciousness. Often they are stored in the deep subconscious. In fact, you might go on discovering more secrets and emotional barriers for much of your remaining life. This is normal. Just add new ones to your list whenever you discover them. Most important is to take action to remove these barriers when you identify them. Identifying barriers means describing them to yourself, for example, "Whenever I receive a compliment from my lover, I get shy and embarrassed and deny the truth of the compliment," or, "When my partner wants to try some new sexual experiment, I say no and suggest something is wrong with him for proposing it."

3. You remove the distance secrets cause by sharing that secret with your lover. You knock down your barricades by altering the protective or dysfunctional behavior associated with the secret. In the example above, instead of denying the compliment, you simply say, "Thank you." Instead of saying no to a sexual experiment, you say yes (despite your emotional discomfort), and you avoid criticizing your lover.

Comments

You will discover that your secrets and barriers do not really protect you. Instead, they lock you in a self-constructed cage that you carry with you everywhere. Keeping secrets and erecting emotional barriers are misguided attempts to control your life, because life inside this cage is lonely and alienated. However, the door of the cage is open. You can actually walk out of jail, into the light and love that is your birthright, any time you choose. You don't have to learn anything new. You dismantle old barriers—let your love out and your lover in. Revealing your secrets is an example of surrendering to your lover by making yourself emotionally vulnerable and transparent.

Magic Wand

Time for Exercise: five to fifteen minutes

Properties Required: magic wand

Steps

1. Make a magic wand from materials you find around the home. Create or use anything, simple or elaborate, but make sure it is beautiful.

2. Take turns with the wand.

3. Say to your lover, "With this wand, I now grant you three wishes of your heart. Each time I touch your head with this wand, make a wish."

4. Share your wishes with your lover if you like.

Comments

This is yet another example of focusing your attention and intention consciously on what you *do* want rather than what you don't want. The more we all do this, the better the world will become.

Soul Freedom Exercises

TO DO ON YOUR OWN

Grounding

Grounding is a simple yet powerful energy connection exercise. Through it, you connect your individual energy flow to the energy flow of Mother Earth. As you tap into this great force of life, you will become calm and revitalized.

Time for Exercise: ten minutes

Properties Required: none

Steps

1. Sit comfortably with your eyes closed, your back straight but not rigid, your shoulders relaxed, your arms at your sides, and your feet flat on the floor.

2. Take several slow deep breaths through your nose.

3. Focus all your attention on your genital region from your tailbone to your pubic bone (that is, your root chakra).

4. Gradually allow an image to form that extends from your genitals to the earth. This can be any image you like, for example, an extension of your flesh, a stream of light, a hollow tube, a tree trunk, or roots.

5. When you have your image formed, picture it reaching from your genitals (your root chakra) all the way down into the very center of the earth. Your connecting image passes through your chair, through the floor, through the ground, through the bedrock, and all the way to the molten core at the heart of Mother Earth.

6. Now, allow any negative energies, any overwhelming sensations you might be experiencing (worry, pain, sadness, hyperactivity, lethargy, anger, and so on), to flow down through your body, through your connecting bridge, and into the earth's core.

7. Imagine these negative energies reaching the center of the earth and being consumed and transformed in a fiery blast. They flow back up to you as Mother Earth energy—calm, strong, full of life.

8. Continue to send overwhelming sensations down to Mother Earth and allow her vitality and serenity to flow up to you through your connecting image. Experience the peacefulness and vigor of grounding.

Comments

As you are grounding, you might notice particular sensations: heat, tingling, color, sound, or light. The importance of this exercise lies in consciously releasing negative energies and absorbing positive ones. If you make this practice a regular habit, you will notice a considerable decrease in your stress level.

Eyes Wide Shut

Your eyes are windows to your soul. Do you allow people in, or do you lock them out?

Time for Exercise: five minutes to one hour (several sessions are an option)
Properties Required: magnifying mirror

Steps

1. Position the light source so it does not shine directly into your eyes. Sit comfortably in front of the magnifying mirror and look very carefully at your eyes.

2. Notice the colors of your eyes. Your eyes are a range of colors, not just one solid color. Notice if your eye colors change from one visual inspection to the next.

3. Try to produce the following "looks" at will. This might require a bit of practice. Add any of your own to the list.

anger	the heat of passion
indifference	dripping with lust
fear	prim and proper
love	innocent
compassion	soft
joy	hard
dismissal, "go away"	closed
welcome, "come near"	open
"I'm happy to see you."	inquisitive
"I'm not happy to see you."	impressed
"I want you sexually."	disappointed
surprised good	seductive
surprised bad	low self-esteem
good girl	contempt
bad girl	guilt
competition	sorrow
cooperation	grief
"I'm better than you."	laughter

4. You might wish to cover the rest of your face below your eyes when you do this exercise so that you are communicating with your eyes only.

5. To get the proper feeling for a particular look, imagine some scenario from your past. When you have recalled the feeling, observe most carefully how your eyes look. Close your eyes. Reopen them and try to reproduce that same look.

Comments

You keep your "eyes wide shut" when you don't know what kind of feeling you are sending out with your eyes energetically, when you refuse to look someone in the eyes, or when you break eye contact out of fear, insecurity, low self-esteem, or indifference. By practicing various looks, you become cognizant of the messages you give with your eyes. You can gain freedom by using your eyes to communicate intimately with full awareness and conscious intention.

SOUL
FREEDOM
EXERCISES
to do
on your own

Biorhythms

Being familiar with your biorhythms can help you make effective decisions.

Time for Exercise: two minutes daily
Properties Required: pen and paper

Steps

Chart your biorhythms by using a scale that goes from minus five to plus five, where minus one is mildly negative and minus five is a vicious bummer state from hell. Plus one is mildly positive, and plus five is joy and bliss supreme. Zero is a neutral state with little feeling either positive or negative.

1. Each day, use the scale to rate your mood.

2. Plot your mood daily for three months to see if you can identify monthly emotional patterns of highs or lows. Such patterns evidence powerful forces, outside of your ego self and independent of the circumstances of your life, that influence your life in predictable ways.

3. Use this information to help you move more smoothly through life. For instance, if you discover the third week of each month is typically a low-energy, bad-mood time, you can avoid important decisions or projects. If possible, make decisions and compete when you are at your peak in the monthly cycle. If you find yourself in arguments and confrontations, stop to notice what time of month it is and act accordingly. For example, go away from the person or situation and come back another time when you have positive feelings.

Comments

For women, you will notice some biorhythm swings that are both related and unrelated to your menstrual cycle. Some men also note more subtle monthly swings.

SOUL
FREEDOM
EXERCISES
*to do
on your own*

135

Floating on Clouds

This simple meditation brings tranquility, healing, and balance as you direct golden energy through the channels of your body, from your head to your feet and back again.

Time for Exercise: five to ten minutes

Properties Required: none

Steps

1. Sit comfortably with your eyes closed, your back straight, and your body relaxed. Touch the roof of your mouth with your tongue. Leave it in this position throughout the exercise. Breathe slowly and deeply through your nose.

2. Picture yourself floating on a soft white cloud. Slowly, the cloud lifts you into the welcoming blue sky. You feel lighter than air as you float higher and higher, cradled in the cloud's soft, fluffy arms. Directly above you, a glowing sun appears. Its light shimmers down to you in cascades of molten gold, like a waterfall of liquid light.

3. You can hear the sound of sweetly flowing water as the golden light spills over the top of your head, down to your eyes, your nose, your mouth, and your chin. Down your throat, your chest, and your solar plexus it flows, bringing warmth and vitality to each cell as it passes.

4. As the golden stream reaches your belly chakra, about 1 to 2 inches (2.5 to 5 centimeters) below your navel, it splits into two bright currents of light that flow simultaneously out to your hips and down the outside of your legs to your feet. Slowly, the molten streams move up the insides of your legs, stroking your knees and brushing your inner thighs. At your genitals, the streams swirl about in delicious golden eddies, then join again to bathe your tailbone in a river of gold. The golden current continues up the center of your spine to the middle of your back, between your shoulder blades.

5. Here the flow of light splits again in two, flowing out and down the outsides of your arms to your hands. Up the insides of your arms, back to your spine between your shoulder blades, the golden streams meet again as one. On up to your shoulders, your neck and the base of your skull, and finally back up to the top of your head it rushes, a liquid lava that bathes your brain and skull in glorious light.

6. Repeat this cycle three, six, or nine times. When you have finished your cycles, sit in stillness for a couple of minutes. Focus on your body. What do you notice?

Better Than I Could Imagine

Time for Exercise: five to fifteen minutes

Properties Required: none

Steps

Set aside some time to recall examples of synchronous events or meaningful coincidences in your life. In particular, identify the good things that both happened to you and in which you also actively participated. Scenarios of such events could unfold something like this:

- You were trying to accomplish something.

- Things didn't go as you planned, and you experienced what seemed like setback, defeat, or failure.

- Right around the corner, something came along that was even better than you could have imagined or have planned for. You received help from outside yourself, out of the mystery, from God or Goddess.

Here is an important example from our lives:

By the mid-1990s, when the college where Al had been an economics professor for twenty-three years offered an early retirement package, he was also involved in what seemed to be a lucrative multilevel marketing business. He accepted the buyout and left the security of his college position.

For several years, Pala, an economic development officer, had been toying with the idea of finding a more satisfying career, but she had taken no action. At the same time Al left teaching, Pala lost her job during a hostile takeover. We began working the marketing business together. It failed miserably. The only successful aspect was a website we developed to sell the products online.

Ours was one of the first small business entrepreneur websites on the Internet, and so we decided to offer Internet training to other small business owners. Although we paid thousands of dollars to reserve workshop facilities, we had no registrations. To avoid complete catastrophe, we chose, at the last minute, to offer relationship and sexuality training instead. Despite having only a few paying customers, as soon as we did the workshop day dedicated to sacred sexuality, we knew it was our calling—this was *it*. Sacred sex had been our private hobby for years. It was our passion and our greatest source of joy, but we had never imagined we could earn a living through it. We now teach and write about sacred sexuality and relationships full time. We discovered how we could follow our bliss and earn a living doing it, and it all came out of what seemed to be a series of failures.

Variations

- Have a conversation in which you and your partner help each other remember the synchronous events or meaningful coincidences that have occurred in your lives.

- Keep a record of these important happenings in your lives and refer to your notes over the years. Is there a pattern in your series of synchronous events?

Comments

Sometimes a sequence of events unfolds (one event leading to the next, or one happening making the next one possible) but not in any recognizable cause-and-effect relationship. Many people believe that synchronicity is just luck or chance. Synchronicity is actually a spiritual process in which our consciousness manifests results according to how we direct our attention and intention and how we act to support our choices.

Both positive and negative stepping stones can lead to a happy final result. In other words, there can be value in having bad things happen to you. Many times, what seems like failure or defeat is really necessary to prevent you from going further down the wrong road. Some doors have to close so that others can open.

SOUL
FREEDOM
EXERCISES
to do
on your own

Soul Freedom Exercises

TO DO TOGETHER

Sacred Space

Changing the atmosphere of the room in which you are going to make love brings magic to your union. It helps elevate regular sex to extraordinary and sacred sex.

Time for Exercise: fifteen minutes

Properties Required: candles, romantic music, plants or fresh flowers, beautiful pieces of fabric, tasty eats and drinks, incense, sensual objects

Steps

1. Make sure the room is tidy—floor swept, laundry out of sight, surfaces dusted.

2. Together, in silence, with your attention focused on making your space beautiful and safe for each other, move slowly and purposefully to arrange the room.

3. Cover hard edges and objects you don't want to see—a TV set, for example—with soft fabrics.

4. Arrange plants, flowers, and beautiful objects around the room.

5. Light candles or change regular light bulbs to red, pink, or magenta bulbs.

6. Set close at hand any massage oils, lubricants, or sex toys you might want to employ.

7. Light incense or heat essential oil diffusers for sensual aroma.

8. Turn on your mood music.

9. Bring in special food and drinks for sharing with your lover.

10. When you've arranged the space to your satisfaction, stand side by side, hold hands, and appreciate the transformation of your room.

11. Look into each other's eyes and softly invite each other to play in your sacred space (see "Permission, Please," page 118).

Comments

Be on the lookout during your daily life for things you can use when you make your sacred space—fabric remnants, sensual books, appealing objects. Start a collection! Then, when you want to create a beautiful room for a special lovemaking time, everything you need will be handy. Each time you make your space, add or change items or arrange things differently so that it remains new and fresh.

Points of Candlelight

Dimming the lights, or turning them off and lighting candles instead, is one of the easiest ways to add romantic ambiance to your lovemaking experience or to change an ordinary dinner into something very sensual. Candles are also one of the most useful aids for creating your own romantic rituals and celebrations. Points of Candlelight is a simple, utterly romantic ritual you can use to help elevate your relationship to a spiritual practice and to send healing energy to those you love and care about.

Time for Exercise: ten minutes

Properties Required: three candles (one larger and two smaller), a beautiful piece of cloth. The larger candle can be any size, from a regular 10- or 12-inch (25–30 centimeters) taper candle to one that is several inches (7.5–15 centimeters) in diameter. The other two candles should be smaller. For example, if you use a 12-inch (30-centimeter) taper for the larger size, use two 6-inch (15-centimeter) candles for the two smaller ones. For your piece of cloth, you can find lovely cloth remnants at fabric stores for just a few dollars.

Steps

1. Select and prepare a special location for placement of your candles, such as a small table, a wide windowsill, or the floor in front of a fireplace or wood stove. Set the space with a beautiful piece of cloth. Place the candles on the cloth.

2. Stand, sit, or kneel in front of your candle arrangement.

3. Light the larger candle. This candle symbolizes the source of all life, light, and love. This candle represents God, Goddess, Cosmic Consciousness, and the Divine.

4. One at a time, light the smaller candles from the larger one. As you pick up your candle and light it from the source, say something such as the following: "This is my light, this is my life. I thank God this day for the gift of living. I thank you, my love, for sharing this life with me, for being at my side to share together our joys and triumphs, our sorrows and pains. Before God as my witness, I pledge my love to you as we grow old together." You might say anything romantic and wonderful that you feel truly expresses your love, devotion, and adoration for each other. You can both say the same words or you can each something completely different.

5. The first person sets his candle down as the other one lights her candle and says her loving, sexy words.

SOUL
FREEDOM
EXERCISES
*to do
together*

Variations

• Add any number of candles (points of light). As you light each one, you can remember your loved ones, someone who has died or is living far away from you, or someone you want to send healing life force to assist.

• Light candles for your enemies, with the intention of healing the separation between you.

• One person alone can easily do these variations.

Comments

To avoid damaging your lovely cloth with dripping wax, you can put sand in an open container, such as a shirt gift-wrapping box with the top removed. You can decorate the box or other container so that it looks beautiful, using colored tape, ribbon, paints, markers, and so on. Place the container on your cloth and place the candles inside the container. If the weather is suitable, consider moving this activity outdoors.

SOUL
FREEDOM
EXERCISES
*to do
together*

142

Harmony Breath

Time for Exercise: five to ten minutes

Properties Required: none

Steps

1. Sit comfortably facing each other.

2. Look into each other's eyes.

3. Inhale and exhale slowly and deeply together, in rhythm.

4. The man leads the rhythm for twelve full breaths as the woman follows by matching her breathing to his.

5. Switch. The woman leads for twelve full breaths as the man follows by matching his breathing to hers.

Variations

• Circular Breathing: As the man inhales, the woman exhales. Follow this circular rhythm for twelve slow, deep breaths. Switch again. The woman sets the rhythm, inhaling while the man exhales for twelve breaths.

• Match your breathing rhythms when you are slow dancing (see "Yin/Yang Yes!," page 119).

Comments

Do not speak during these exercises. Just be present in the moment. There is nothing to do, nowhere to get to, nothing to explain.

These breathing techniques are excellent ways to begin lovemaking. They effectively stop the world, helping you let go of the demands of your busy lives and become grounded in the present moment together. At peaks of sexual arousal, gazing into each other's eyes and breathing in unison takes your connection out of this world (see "Yab-Yum Yum," page 150). Breathing in harmony is also an excellent way to bridge from arguing to making up.

SOUL
FREEDOM
EXERCISES
*to do
together*

143

The End Comes First

"The end comes first" means that your consciousness tends to manifest (bring into reality) that which you focus your attention on and think about. By having a clear picture in your mind of what you want the end result to be, you greatly increase your chances of getting it.

Time for Exercise: five to fifteen minutes

Properties Required: none

Steps

1. At the start of lovemaking, take a few minutes to imagine how you want the experience to unfold.

2. Allow some images of the two of you being very passionate, very active, very still, and very satisfied to linger in your imagination.

3. Pay particular attention to the image of the two of you lying in love's blush, all aglow after your sacred loving.

Comments

You can use this simple technique for manifesting results in all areas of your life, regardless of importance.

SOUL
FREEDOM
EXERCISES
*to do
together*

Flow in the Glow

Time for Exercise: fifteen minutes

Properties Required: none

Steps

1. Take turns describing for your lover a peak experience that you have had: an experience of feeling connected to everything, an experience of superb confidence and mastery, an experience of profound synchronicity, a magical experience, or an experience of unconditional love given or received.

2. In your description, include various details:

   Where were you?
   When did it happen?
   What you were doing at the time?
   What were your sensory perceptions during the experience?
   What insights did the experience give you?
   What did you learn from it?
   How did it change your life?

Sacraments of Our Lives

Traditionally defined as the outward and visible sign of an inner and invisible grace, a sacrament is something you elevate to the status of holy or sacred. You elevate it to this status by your choice and intention—you don't need anyone else's permission to do this.

Time for Exercise: fifteen minutes to one hour

Properties Required: none

Steps

1. Describe to each other examples of events or experiences that are sacraments in your relationship together.

2. Discuss what makes them worthy of their status as a sacrament. Are they one-time events, or do you repeat any of them occasionally or regularly?

Comments

Marriage is widely recognized and treated as a sacrament. Have you considered renewing your vows in an annual ceremony to honor this sacrament? A vows ceremony, whether you are legally married or living common-law, is a wonderful sacrament for lovers (see "Vows," page 169). Lovemaking itself is a joyous, holy sacrament, if you treat it that way. Start by declaring your intention to elevate your lovemaking to sacred sex. Proceed to create a sacred loving space (see "Sacred Space," page 140). Follow any of the many excellent Tantric or Taoist sacred loving guides, for example, our book *Soul Sex: Tantra for Two*.

An act of forgiveness to your lover can be a sacrament as well as an act of kind generosity in which you make great personal sacrifice for the well-being of your lover and your relationship.

Kundalini Caresses

Your chakras (energy centers along the spine) exert a powerful influence on your physical, mental, and spiritual well-being. This simple ceremony sends loving energy into each center. With your tender touch, arouse the kundalini (cosmic energy that lies dormant at the base of the spine, coiled like a snake). Channel it upward through the chakra centers for blissful awakening.

Time for Exercise: five to thirty minutes

Properties Required: none

Steps

Take turns giving each other kundalini caresses. There are three variations to the caresses, using hands, lips, and tongues. You can perform the exercise on both the front and back of the body.

1. Make sure the room is warm, and get naked together.

2. Locate the seven chakra points on the body.
   - Genitals, from the coccyx around to the pubic mound
   - Belly, about two finger widths below the navel
   - Solar plexus, at the point of the breastbone just below where the ribs meet
   - Center of the chest, between the breasts
   - Center of the throat
   - Center of the forehead
   - Crown of the head

3. In the first variation, run your hands up the back of your lover's body, stopping briefly at each chakra point to allow your energy (in the form of heat and subtle current) to enter the body. Focus on sending love and healing through your hands.

4. In the second variation, kiss your lover's body all along the line connecting the chakra points, stopping briefly at each point to perform a very soft hickey by sucking on that point gently. Do not suck so hard that you leave marks. Let your desire flow through your mouth.

5. In the third variation, run your tongue along your lover's body, stopping briefly at each point to rotate your tongue first counterclockwise three times, then clockwise three times.

6. Repeat these variations along the front of your lover's body.

7. Reverse roles. The partner who first gave the caresses will now receive them.

Foundation Stones

On a level of consciousness much deeper than the rational, you must come to believe that you have a purpose for being here, that you are capable of knowing your life's mission, and that you have all you need to express your greatness and accomplish even the miraculous. This simple ceremony can help you acquire this vital wisdom.

Time for Exercise: thirty minutes, fifteen for each lover

Properties Required: seven stones of different colors: red, orange, yellow, green, blue, purple, and white (or clear). Polished stones purchased from a gem shop are best, but many items commonly available around the house will be suitable substitutes. Most important is that you have seven of the same type of object, one each in the seven different colors. Other suitable small objects include pieces of glass or smooth plastic, flowers, scarves (or other pieces of colored cloth), and fruit.

Steps

1. Your partner lies naked on her back.

2. Place the stones on her body at the chakra points in the following order, one at a time:

   - Red stone on her mound of pubic hair
   - Orange stone on the belly about two finger widths below her navel
   - Yellow stone at the solar plexus, at the point of the breastbone just below where the ribs meet
   - Green stone between her breasts
   - Blue stone at the center of her throat
   - Purple stone in the center of her forehead
   - White or clear stone near the crown of her head

   As you are placing the stones, say something such as this:

   > "As I place these stones upon your naked body, the energy of love moves freely in and out of you."

   When all of the stones are in place, say something such as this:

   > "All of the foundation stones are in place, and your entire body will vibrate in harmony with your purpose in life. You are now empowered to accomplish your life's mission. These stones are symbolic of your foundation in this world, on this planet, and in this life. From this secure platform, you may go forth inspired to express your greatness, to experience and accomplish wondrous things."

3. Repeat the exercise for the other partner.

Comments

Focus *all* of your attention on each chakra center as you place the stones, remembering your intention of love and power. When you are the receiving partner, allow each center to open to the loving touch and energetic intention of your lover.

Yab-Yum Yum

The Tibetan Buddhist term yab-yum *translates as father/mother, masculine/feminine, or yang/yin. Yab-yum is the ultimate Tantric lovemaking position because it is ideal for sharing energy.*

Time for Exercise: five minutes to one hour
Properties Required: each other

Steps

In the yab-yum sexual position, the woman straddles the man as he sits cross-legged on the floor in the lotus position. He might have cushions under his knees for support and comfort, especially if he wants to maintain the position for more than a few minutes. Very firm Indian-style pillows work perfectly. Alternatively, he might sit on a straight-backed chair, and she will climb on top.

The lovers face each other with their eyes open. They harmonize their breathing (see "Harmony Breath," page 143). They can kiss, touching their tongues together. The eyes, breath, and tongues act as energy switches that connect the flow of hot sexual energy between the two lovers' bodies.

1. Build to a peak of sexual arousal using any other sexual positions or techniques, but do not climax.

2. Assume the yab-yum position and become still.

3. Pass energy through your genital contact, eyes, breathing, and tongues.

4. Move the sexual energy up through your bodies using PC pumping (squeezing the genital muscles as if you were stopping the flow of urine in midstream—see "Fit for Sex," page 55), eye gazing, harmonized breathing, and French kissing (with tongue contact), running your hands up and down the front or back of your lover's body while barely touching the skin.

5. Exchange the energy between you by visualizing it moving in a figure 8 or the infinity symbol (∞). The energy moves up his back, transfers into her mouth, moves down her front and then up her back, transfers into his mouth, moves down his front and then up his back, and so on.

6. Send energy back and forth with your eyes, with circular harmonized breathing (he breathes in while she breathes out, and vice versa), and by touching your tongues together.

7. Try chanting in this position. The sounds you make will be extremely beautiful, animated by the high charge of hot sexual energy.

8. If the man's erection subsides and you wish to resurrect it, rock back and forth a few times and breathe rapidly to rebuild excitement.

9. Resume other lovemaking positions without breaking genital contact by rolling forward, backward, or to either side.

SOUL
FREEDOM
EXERCISES
to do
together

Once Before I Die . . .

The soul exists beyond time and space, beyond the life and death of the body. For the soul, death is merely a doorway from one place to another, not something to fear and avoid. But while we are in a body, we are loath to think about leaving it. This simple exercise is a way for you to bring the subject of death gently into your consciousness without raising fear, so that death becomes a valuable advisor. No one gets out of life alive. As the realization dawns that someday you too will die, you find a powerful motivation to live now. By focusing on what you want, you will feel truly alive.

This very simple exercise helps you quickly identify some things that matter to you but that you might never have previously given yourself permission to strive for.

Time for Exercise: five minutes

Properties Required: none

Steps

Each partner simply completes this sentence any number of times, but at least once:

"Once before I die . . ."

Comments

It is not required as part of the exercise that you do anything with your statements of desire. Once a desire has been spoken out loud, however, it has been given life, and you might be surprised at how you begin to mobilize your resources to move toward full realization of your desire. You might also be astonished at how quickly the universe comes to your assistance.

SOUL
FREEDOM
EXERCISES
*to do
together*

152

Break Out of Jail

Feeling stuck? It's time to break out of confinement and be free.

Time for Exercise: ten to thirty minutes

Properties Required: large roll of wrapping paper

Steps

1. One of you wraps the other in gift-wrapping paper.

2. The one who is wrapped breaks out of his confinement.

3. Switch roles. The other person gets wrapped and breaks out.

Comments

Most often, our sense of confinement is completely self-imposed. This exercise symbolizes breaking free of self-constructed prisons of conditioned thought and beliefs.

SOUL
FREEDOM
EXERCISES
*to do
together*

Pearls of Wisdom

Time for Exercise: five to fifteen minutes

Properties Required: none

Steps

1. Once per week, sit down together and share two or three inspiring thoughts or quotes you have gathered over the previous days.

2. Explain why you have chosen the items you present.

3. From time to time, slip in one of your own quotations. See if your lover can pick out yours from the others. If you do this, don't share the authors' names until the end of the exercise.

Comments

Add this as one of your activities during sacred loving times. You can find lots of quotes from books at the public library or by searching on the Internet.

SOUL
FREEDOM
EXERCISES
to do
together

The Circle

What is left unsaid?

In the book Mutant Message Down Under, *by Marlo Morgan, a doctor working with an indigenous tribe asked the people to name their physician or medicine person. The villagers replied that no one person played that role because everyone shared in it. They further explained that when the village dealt with sickness, the patient would sit in their midst as they formed a circle. A spokesperson would ask the patient, "What has been left unsaid?" Everyone would then wait until the patient found the words and said what had been unsaid. Sometimes the villagers would wait for days. Remarkably, their cure rate was 98 percent.*[1]

Time for Exercise: as long as it takes

Properties Required: a circle of friends or acquaintances

Steps

Form a circle around a sick person and do as the villagers described above do. Have someone ask the patient, "What has been left unsaid?" Then wait . . .

Integration Exercises
TO DO ON YOUR OWN

Dance Your Prayer

Time for Exercise: five to fifteen minutes

Properties Required: selection of music for dancing

Steps

1. Select music for the mood you wish to create, anything from gospel to rock and roll.

2. Imagine a conversation you'd like to have with God, which would include, for example, something you wish to thank God for, something you are angry with God about, something you wish to ask God for, or something you want to offer God.

3. Turn on the music and express your prayer nonverbally through body movements.

4. Dance until your inner guide says you are finished.

Variation

Do this with your lover, both of you dancing the same or different prayers.

Comments

Since you might dance for a short or long time, be prepared with a selection of music an hour or more in length.

What's Good?

Be careful what you pay attention to, because you are going to get more of it. You can help people focus on what they do want by asking them the simple question, "What's good?"

Time for Exercise: one minute

Properties Required: none

Steps

1. The next time you greet someone, forego usual greetings such as "How are you?" or "How's it going?" or "What's new?" Instead, ask, "What's good?"

2. Suggest to everyone you know that they start asking others this simple question.

Comments

If you pay attention to how people use language, you will notice that they often phrase responses in negative terms. For example, if you ask someone, "How are you today?" the most frequent response seems to be "Not bad." If you ask, "How is everything?" they might say, "It could be worse." When people talk about what they want, they often mention what they don't want. For example, "I sure hope I don't get that flu going around," or "I don't want to be sick," or "I don't want to be poor," or "I hope my husband is not fooling around on me."

Generally, your consciousness works to create more of what you pay attention to. When you pay attention to what you don't want, there is a good chance you are going to get not less but more of it. So pay attention to what you *do* want. For example, "I want to be healthy," or "I want to have lots of money," or "I want a relationship based on trust and commitment."

Leap of Imagination

Beliefs are extremely powerful but not supremely powerful. There is something more powerful than beliefs. Otherwise, no one could ever transcend their limited beliefs and become unstuck. Your imagination is more powerful than your beliefs only if used in a particular way. The process is simple.

Time for Exercise: five minutes

Properties Required: none

Steps

1. Pick an image of the end result you wish to create. If your end result is complex, use a visual symbol to represent it.

2. Be aware of your current situation, especially any existing negative beliefs that might be limiting your vision.

3. Make your limiting beliefs part of your "starting from" picture.

4. Compare your "end result" picture with your "starting from" picture.

5. Choose to have the end result that you desire.

6. Drop the "starting from" picture.

7. Send the "end result" picture out into the cosmos.

Comments

Perform this exercise during any meditation practice, or by itself.

The Meaning of Life

A primary function of consciousness is to bestow meaning, to decide what things mean for you personally. Examples include deciding how important something is to you regardless of its importance to someone else, how something ranks in priority compared with other things in your life, and whether you will spend time, money, or energy on something. Someone can spend an entire lifetime in search of the meaning of life and never find it, primarily because there is no meaning inherent in life. Instead, each of us, in an act of free will, decides what our lives mean and what is meaningful in our lives. Finding the meaning in your life is primarily a decision and only secondarily a search. Searching leads to a decision more than to a discovery.

It makes sense that the meaning or purpose of your life lies in pursuing something you love to do that is also of service to others and to God. Doing what you love to do, serving others, and earning a living at the same time comprise "following your bliss." In this exercise, you reflect on what you love most to do, with a view to deciding eventually what your bliss is and at that time taking action to follow it.

Time for Exercise: five minutes to one hour

Properties Required: pen and paper (optional)

Steps

1. Think about things you love to do.

2. Which one jumps out at you as the one thing you love most?

3. Allow your imagination to play with possibilities whereby you could earn a living doing the thing you love. Don't worry if you can't think of any.

4. Ask yourself, "If I could make a living doing [whatever it is you most love to do], would I do it?"

5. Answer "yes," and let that work deep into your consciousness.

6. Remain alert for opportunities that present themselves for you to follow your bliss, to be of service, and to earn a living. They will.

Variation

With a partner, take turns exploring, with and for each other, what you love to do. Just talking about it unleashes your creative power. Remember: Pay attention to what you pay attention to, because you are going to get more of it.

Dream Time

Not only can you remember your dreams and interpret their meanings, but you can also influence dreams with your intention through conscious dreaming. This exercise focuses on the first part of conscious dreaming, setting a theme for your dreaming before you go to sleep. (The second part of conscious dreaming is to participate actively in the dream while the dream unfolds, but that is beyond the scope of this exercise.)

Time for Exercise: three minutes

Properties Required: pen and paper

Steps

1. Choose a question you want answered or an issue about which you want guidance.

2. Write your choice on a piece of paper.

3. Before you go to sleep, read your question.

4. Place the paper under your pillow.

5. Hold your question in your consciousness as you drift off to sleep.

Comments

If you wake in the night with insights, write them down immediately. Alternatively, write down any insights as soon as you wake up. Write them down even if they don't seem to make any sense at the time. Allow what you have written and what you can remember to percolate through your consciousness over the next day or two. Often you will grasp exactly what needs to be done.

Out of Body

Time for Exercise: five to thirty minutes

Properties Required: none

Steps

Each evening, as you prepare to sleep, give your deeper consciousness instructions for going out of your body.

1. Relax your body completely.

2. Quiet your mind with a meditative practice.

3. Reassure your ego self that you will be safe while you travel and that you can return to your body whenever you wish to by associating your return with some simple action such as moving your arms or legs.

4. Visualize your consciousness rolling out of your physical body in a transparent body double. This self can travel through matter and instantaneously traverse any distance. This self can move freely about in time, space, and alternate dimensions. As your transparent self leaves, it can look back and see your regular physical body at rest.

5. Give your deep consciousness instructions that you wish to travel out of your body, to remain conscious during the experience, and to remember it afterward.

Variation

Do this with your lover and agree to meet somewhere in your out-of-body state.

Comments

Separating your consciousness from your physical body with full awareness is perhaps the best possible preparation for crossing the barrier between life and death. If your consciousness can leave the body, what does that mean about death? If the body dies, can consciousness just leave the body and not return? Would you assume that consciousness dies with the physical body? The real challenge is to remain aware of personal identity as consciousness separates from physical reality. Out-of-body experiences (OBEs) seem to be the perfect training to do this. Other practices that require similar skills are remote viewing, astral projection, and lucid dreaming.

Looking Back

Time for Exercise: fifteen minutes to one hour

Properties Required: pen and paper

Steps

1. Write out what different loved ones and friends might say at your funeral.

2. Write out what you would *like* them to say about you and use this as a guide for how you intend to live your life.

Variation

Ask your lover to write a eulogy for you and read it out to you.

Comments

Eulogies for the dead are often poignantly beautiful. Wouldn't you find it interesting to know what your lover and other loved ones would say about you *before* you die? This exercise can be extraordinarily powerful if you allow yourself to feel the emotion. When your heart is open, this exercise can change how you live forever after.

INTEGRATION
EXERCISES
to do
on your own

Now and Zen

A variation of Buddhism that asserts that enlightenment can come through intuitive insight, Zen is the simplest, most direct route to enlightenment—but one of the most difficult to traverse. In Zen, there is nothing to find, nothing to discover, nothing to learn, nothing to remember, nowhere to go, nothing at all to do. How difficult is that? Most difficult.

Time for Exercise: one minute to eternity

Properties Required: none

Steps

• Sit comfortably (or uncomfortably) in complete silence. Just stay there until you get it!

• An option: Vow to continue sitting until you become enlightened or until you die.

• Another option: When ready, begin. When thirsty, drink. When hungry, eat. When tired, sleep. When curious, look. When afraid, tremble. When happy, smile. When finished, stop.

Variation

Try sitting together and employing this option: Ask your lover to give you a whack upside the head—not too hard, but hard enough to jolt you out of your train of thought.

Comments

"There's no Dharma [the way of higher truths] outside, and even what is on the inside can't be grasped. You get taken up with the words from my mouth, but it would be better if you stopped all that and did nothing. Things already under way, don't go on with them. Things not yet under way, don't let them get under way. That's better for you than ten years traveling around on pilgrimages.

"The way I see it, there's no call for anything special. Just act ordinary, put on your clothes, eat your rice, pass the time doing nothing. You who come from here and there, you all have a mind to do something. You search for Buddha, search for the Dharma, search for emancipation, search for a way to get out of the threefold world. Idiots, trying to get out of the threefold world! Where will you go?"[1] —Lin-chi I-hsuan (d. 866)

Integration Exercises
TO DO TOGETHER

Stretching Your Limits

Yoga means "union." Yoga postures work your body, focus your mind, and build your life force. When done in tune with a partner, they also strengthen your heart connection.

Time for Exercise: three minutes—longer the first time you do it

Properties Required: clothing you can stretch comfortably in

Steps

1. Stand facing each other at a distance of about 4 feet (1.2 meters).

2. Place your feet together, hang your arms gently at your sides, hold your back straight but not rigid, relax your shoulders, loosen your throat, and make your eyes soft.

3. Make loving eye contact with your partner.

4. Inhale slowly through your nose and, as you are inhaling, gracefully raise your arms straight out to your sides at shoulder level, palms up.

5. Exhaling gradually, bring your hands together in front of your chest, palms touching.

6. Slowly inhale while raising your arms straight up over your head, palms facing each other, hands shoulder width apart.

7. Exhaling slowly, reach out toward your partner. Folding at your hips, bend over and grasp each other's arms above the elbows.

8. Your head and neck should be relaxed, hanging loose.

9. Continue to hold each other's arms as you lean back away from each other.

10. With legs flexed, feel each other's weight. Feel your spine extending and your legs stretching. Relax your muscles into this posture. Hold for a measured count of twenty.

11. Gradually come forward again. Release your partner's arms and straighten to the upright position.

12. Make loving eye contact.

13. Slowly inhale and raise your arms above your head.

14. Repeat steps 7 through 13 twice.

15. Complete your practice by exhaling unhurriedly, bringing your arms down and your hands together in front of your chest, palms touching.

16. Say "thank you" aloud to each other.

Comments

Endeavor to move very slowly through this exercise with intense focus on your own graceful body movements and on being very aware of working in unison with your partner. Attempt to breathe in time together (see "Harmony Breath," page 143). A guide for inhalation is a count of seven, and for exhalation, ten. Do not stretch farther than is comfortable. Do not strain.

INTEGRATION
EXERCISES
to do
together

"O" Zone

The "O" Zone is the ecstatic orgasmic energy state you are in at peaks of sexual arousal before climax. Your personal power is greatly amplified when you are supercharged energetically in the "O" Zone. This is the perfect time for you to visualize your goals, visions, and dreams. Such a visioning process is "sexual magic," because the results can be so remarkable and dramatic.

Time for Exercise: fifteen minutes to one hour for lovemaking, and one minute to send the vision

Properties Required: none

Steps

1. Build to a peak of sexual arousal, but don't climax.

2. While coasting along absorbed in ecstatic energy, send out your vision into the universe.

3. Each partner might send out an individual vision, or you might agree ahead of time to send out a shared vision, for instance, of your relationship.

Variation

You can do this on your own while self-pleasuring.

Comments

"Send out" means to create an image that symbolizes your vision or goal and see it go flying off into space.

Vows

Greatness, beauty, and creation spring forth from commitment. Saying yes unreservedly to your lover, burning all bridges of escape, giving everything you have, and holding nothing back bring you to the very edge of life unfolding. These affirmations give you the courage to take the leap of faith beyond the familiarity of your ego and over the edge. You fly in glorious freedom. This simple ceremony makes your commitment real and alive. You can feel it. It will feed you with strength in times of need, putting you in touch with your higher self if you surrender and allow it.

Time for Exercise: ten to thirty minutes

Properties Required: none. Nothing is required. Your words spoken with sincerity and deep feeling will be enough, but optional items can add power, excitement, and fun to the exercise, bringing you deeper into the mystery. You might wish to set up a sacred space for your ceremony (see "Sacred Space," page 140), incorporating any or all of the following items: costumes (cloaks, masks, and gaudy jewelry); makeup; hats or headdresses; scarves and shawls; a Tibetan singing bowl, drums, rattles, or other musical instruments or noise-makers; sacramental wine and goblets (silver or crystal); a pin to prick your fingers for blood bonding; photos from your wedding or another intensely romantic occasion; a selection of mysterious, passionate music; sensual food snacks or a complete gourmet lunch or dinner; beautiful pieces of colorful cloth; a selection of semiprecious or polished stones; fireworks or sparklers; and a bonfire. You might also include ritual acts such as drinking from the same goblet, exchanging small tokens of love, or mingling your blood from pricked fingers. Let your imagination go.

Steps

1. Each prepares his or her vows in advance.

2. When it is your turn to say your vows, allow yourself to be fully present. Take your time and speak with your heart wide open.

Comments

You might also go to a special spot outside, a place of beauty that you have visited together as lovers, perhaps a place where you will be completely alone so that in privacy you can consummate your vows with passionate lovemaking.

Sounds of Silence

Time for Exercise: full day
Properties Required: none

Steps

1. Designate one day as a "Day of Silence."

2. Shut off the phone and don't answer the door. You might post a note on your door that says you are not available.

3. Go through the entire day, from when you wake in the morning until you go to sleep at night, without speaking a single word to each other, but be fully present together in this space of silence you have created.

4. Don't ignore each other, but interact physically, sexually, and so on without talking. Communicate in any nonverbal ways you can imagine, but try to avoid a lot of note writing back and forth.

5. The next day, have a conversation about your experience:

   What were you thinking and feeling?
   Was it difficult or easy?
   What insights did you have?
   What did you learn about yourself?
   What did you learn about your lover?

Comments

You can do this exercise alone, but there is something very magical about being present with your lover in complete silence for a whole day.

Seeing in the Dark

The lights went out. Only then could we see without our eyes.

Al Link

Time for Exercise: all day and night (short variation: one hour or more)
Properties Required: blindfold

Steps

1. One lover puts on a blindfold as soon as she wakes up and keeps it on until the next morning.

2. Her partner, who is not wearing a blindfold, acts as a guide for her when she requests his assistance. On another day, he will wear the blindfold.

Variations

• Condense the exercise into one hour.

• Get up and walk through the house in complete darkness in the middle of the night.

• Walk around outside on the darkest of nights, when there is no moonlight or artificial light nearby. Pack a flashlight for emergencies.

Comments

This exercise forces you to rely on senses other than sight. You might be amazed at how much you rely on sight for so many things. You might also be amazed at how many things you can do for yourself without being able to see. This exercise also forces you to be vulnerable to your lover. You must surrender and allow yourself to be cared for. This is a spiritual exercise. Something about being deprived of sight gives you the opportunity to go more deeply inside to the quiet center of the cyclone of your consciousness.

INTEGRATION
EXERCISES
*to do
together*

Mystical Maps

Time for Exercise: fifteen minutes

Properties Required: none

Steps

Take turns describing for your lover the qualities or properties of a mystical experience you have had. Use the following questions as guidelines for your explanation:

What were the properties of time and space?

Was there time travel?

Was there space travel?

Did the experience carry religious significance or meaning for you?

Did you perceive any direct contact with the Divine, with God or Goddess?

Was there any contact with the dead, spirits, or ghosts?

Could you travel through matter?

Did you experience any forms of ESP (extrasensory perception), such as telepathy?

Did you access esoteric knowledge, wisdom, or "knowing" or "seeing" in unusual ways?

Did you have an experience in which the normal boundary defining yourself was transcended, that is, you could not tell where you ended and what used to be not-you began?

Did you feel a profound sense of love, well-being, peace, or safety?

Did you have a sense of returning "home?"

Did you have a sense that everything was complete and perfect just as it is?

Did you experience ecstasy, joy, or bliss?

Under the Sky

Time for Exercise: fifteen minutes to overnight

Properties Required: sleeping bags, a bit of research beforehand (optional) to identify some of the constellations of stars that can be seen in your location at the present season of the year

Steps

1. Lie out under the stars when the sky is clear and you are away from other sources of light, for instance, on a beach away from the city. (If possible, sleep out under the stars.) Orient yourselves and work together to locate any constellations you can identify.

2. Know that you are part of this wondrous vastness. You belong here. You have something to do while you are here. Ask your higher self, "What is my purpose in being in this body, on this planet Earth, at this time in history?"

3. Ask your higher self, "What is it that I most love to do?"

4. Imagine how the thing you most love to do and the thing you were sent here to accomplish are somehow the same thing.

5. Ask your higher self for guidance when you go to sleep: "How can I use what I most love to do to fulfill my purpose in life?"

Comments

The universe or cosmos contains everything that exists. The universe is believed to "vibrate" out of "strings." According to Dan Falk, "Each string is as small compared to an atom as an atom is compared to the solar system."[2] The average galaxy contains about 200 billion (200,000 million) stars. Our Milky Way galaxy is one of hundreds of billions of galaxies in the universe. As you stare out at the stars and the vastness of the night sky, ponder the concept of infinity. Infinity means no beginning and no end. Infinity goes smaller than you can imagine. Infinity is larger than you can conceive.

Together Forever

Lifelong commitment normally means growing old together. Think and talk together about how your relationship will mature as your age advances.

Time for Exercise: five to thirty minutes

Properties Required: photograph of an older couple

Steps

1. Sit down with your lover and allow your imagination to conjure up images of what your life will be like as you grow old together:

   - Consider your health status. Visualize how your bodies will look.

   - Visualize the activities you will be engaged in, especially those you do as a couple. Will you be sexually active? What form will sex take? What creative pursuits will you enjoy? What accomplishments will you look back on with satisfaction and pride?

   - Where will you live? What will your financial status be? What will be happening in your family?

   - Imagine all of the ways you will have helped to make the world a better place.

2. Frame and display your photograph as a visual symbol of the life you choose to create together as you age.

Floating Lights

Candles are one of the most useful aids for creating your own romantic rituals and celebrations, for remembering loved ones you cannot be with right now, and for healing the separation between enemies.

Time for Exercise: ten minutes

Properties Required: a number of small candles (birthday candles are about the right size), the same number of small flat-bottom paper bags, the same number of small paper plates, and one or more larger candles for dripping wax onto the inside bottoms of the bags to attach the smaller candles

Steps

1. Open the paper bags. Use the larger candles to drip wax into the paper bags. Secure one birthday candle upright inside each paper bag. Place each bag onto one of the paper plates.

2. When all of the bags and candles are ready, light the candles one at a time.

3. Set the plate afloat in a tub, pool, lake, or river while saying a dedication to a friend or loved one, speaking aloud words of encouragement for a cause you are committed to, or offering amnesty to an enemy.

4. Silently watch the floating lights carry your message, wish, and energy out into the universe.

Variations

Ceremony for Integrating the Four Freedoms: Body, Mind, Heart, and Soul

Use four candles, bags, and plates. Prepare them by following the above instructions. As you light each one, read together the statements you have prepared in advance, dedicating a light to each of the Four Freedoms. Here are examples of what you could say for each of the Four Freedoms:

Body Freedom

"With this light, we invite our bodies to awaken. We choose to open our senses completely. We welcome the freedom of sensual pleasure and sexual fulfillment."

Mind Freedom

"With this light, we accept the responsibility to pay attention to what we think about and how we think about it. We choose to pay attention to what we *do* want. We choose to think about what we *do* want in positive and supportive ways."

Heart Freedom

"With this light, we pledge to open our hearts to each other, again and again each time they close. We pledge to allow ourselves to feel everything, both positive and negative feelings. We choose to act with courage to support creating what truly matters to us. We make a commitment to do our inner work to become fit for our relationship."

Soul Freedom

"With this light, we confirm and renew our faith that, by being of service to God and the world, we will be assisted to overcome all obstacles. We will accomplish and experience wondrous things. We will sleep secure, act with courage, and celebrate with joy as we live this wondrous life together."

Other Variations

• Use five lights dedicated to the five senses (taste, smell, sight, hearing, and touch).

• Use four lights to symbolize the compass directions and to call on their power.

• Use as many candles as the number of your anniversary or birthday, the number of your children, and so on.

Comments

If you use large candles and large paper bags, the floating lights will burn much longer and will require your attention so that the bags don't float away and create a fire hazard. It is relatively safe to use small birthday candles because they burn out so quickly. Do not use tea lights outdoors because their metal cups contaminate the environment when they sink.

The First Freedom: Body

1. Oliver, "Wild Geese."

2. Starhawk, *The Spiral Dance*, 104.

3. McCracken, *New Atlas of Human Anatomy*, 36–41, 128–132; and Intellimed International Corporation, "Human Anatomy Online."

4. During the sixth and fifth centuries BCE, Classical Greek idealists such as Heraclitus popularized the concept *soma semá*, which suggests the body is a tomb or prison from which one must escape in order to realize spiritual salvation. This notion, shared by Pythagoreanism, Orphism, and mystery religions, directly influenced early Christianity, particularly through St. Paul and St. Clement.

5. National Association of Anorexia Nervosa and Associated Disorders (ANAD), "Facts about Eating Disorders."

6. American Society for Aesthetic Plastic Surgery (ASAPS), "Cosmetic Surgery Quick Facts: 2005 ASAPS Statistics." Complete survey data, including downloadable graphs, are available in the press center of the ASAPS website: http://www.surgery.org/press/statistics-2005.php.

7. This quote comes from ABC's application instructions for *Extreme Makeover*: http://abc.go.com/primetime/extrememakeover/casting.html.

8. Spitz, *The First Year of Life*. In studies Dr. René Spitz conducted during the 1940s at a foundling home, he documented that infants who received minimal stimulation from the social and physical environment (those isolated in cribs with little or no physical touching or affection) could die from an emotional wasting away he called *marasmus*, despite hygienic surroundings, a nourishing diet, and normal medical and physical care.

9. Prescott, "The Origins of Human Love and Violence," 143–188; "Body Pleasure and the Origins of Violence"; and "Anti-Social, Aggressive and Violence-Related Behaviors and Their Consequences."

10. Blanchflower and Oswald, "Money, Sex and Happiness: An Empirical Study."

11. Donnelly, et al., "Involuntary Celibacy: A Life Course Analysis," 159.

The Second Freedom: Mind

1. Pert, *Molecules of Emotion*. Under our old medical model, the brain was considered to operate exclusively with an electrical communication process, in which neurotransmitters released from nerve endings in the brain jumped across synapses (tiny spaces between neurons) from one neuron to another, carrying information. In this old model, the body only exists to carry the head around. The body is dumb matter, taking orders from the intelligent brain, the director of everything that goes on in either the head or the body. However, based on discoveries in the 1980s by Candace B. Pert, Ph.D., and her colleagues, we now know that the brain also uses a chemical process. A continuous information-sharing process occurs between the brain, central nervous system, endocrine system, gastrointestinal system, and immune system. This biochemical process (relying upon receptors and ligands) is a two-way, nonhierarchical process that influences and/or controls all functions of the body. In this model, neurotransmitters are understood to be another kind of ligand. According to Pert, "less than 2 percent of neuronal (brain-centered) communication actually occurs at the synapse" (ibid., 139). So the chemical (nonsynaptic) brain seems to be far more important than the electrical one. While the electrical brain is located in the head, the chemical brain, the entire network of receptors and ligands, exists in the brain as well as throughout the rest of the body, connecting all body systems into one indivisible whole.

2. Bloom, "The History of the Global Brain."

The Third Freedom: Heart

1. Heartbeat 2000, "Heart of the Matter."

2. Desikachar and Cravens, *Health, Healing and Beyond*. American and European medical experts have documented the Yogi Krishnamacharya's astonishing ability to stop both his heartbeat and his breath—essentially to control the life process itself.

3. Pert, *Molecules of Emotion*, 23. Dr. Pert, a research professor in the Department of Biophysics and Physiology at Georgetown University School of Medicine, reports on research findings and practical applications to body-mind medicine for health and happiness. She began her research as a medical graduate student at Johns Hopkins University in the early 1970s. From 1975 through 1987, Pert headed a team of researchers at the National Institutes of Health (NIH), the United States government's premiere biomedical research establishment. During her tenure there, she published over two hundred scientific papers.

4. Ibid., 192–193.

5. Ibid., 104.

6. Ornish, *Love and Survival*, 23–71.

7. Prescott, "Anti-Social, Aggressive and Violence-Related Behaviors and Their Consequences."

8. Campbell, *The Hero's Journey*, 73.

9. Armstrong, "Joseph Campbell Foundation Myth Letter."

10. Prescott, "Body Pleasure and the Origins of Violence," 11.

11. Campbell, *The Hero with a Thousand Faces*, 25.

12. Carse, *Finite and Infinite Games*.

13. Campbell, *The Power of Myth*.

The Fourth Freedom: Soul

1. Pert, *Molecules of Emotion*, 312.

2. Watts, *Cloud-Hidden*, 65.

3. Emerson, "The Over-Soul."

4. Although these teachings are contained in many of Castaneda's books, the following three volumes express them best: *The Teachings of Don Juan: A Yaqui Way of Knowledge*, *A Separate Reality: Further Conversations with Don Juan*, and *Journey to Ixtlan*.

Integrating Your Four Freedoms

1. Osho, *From Sex to Superconsciousness*.

2. Falk, *Universe on a T-Shirt*, 131. A bizarre example of superposition of states was recorded in the year 2000 when "physicists at a laboratory in Colorado zapped a beryllium atom with a laser beam, momentarily putting the atom's outermost electron in two quantum states at once. One 'copy' of the electron was spinning one way; its twin was spinning the opposite way. The proof that superposition occurred is that two copies of the electron interfered with each other, creating a tell-tale signature" (ibid., 135).

3. Ibid., 135. In 1998, researchers Max Tegmark and John Wheeler at the University of Geneva, Switzerland, "produced a pair of entangled photons. Measuring the energy of one of the photons determined the energy of the other, even though it was 10 kilometers away." Summing up their experiments in a *Scientific American* article, Tegmark and Wheeler declared "the weirdness of the quantum world is real, whether we like it or not" (ibid., 136).

4. Ibid., 127.

5. Ibid., 150.

6. Gross, "A World of Strings."

7. Ibid.

8. Puthoff, "CIA-Initiated Remote Viewing at Stanford Research Institute."

9. Goswami, *The Self-Aware Universe*, 136.

10. Ibid., 48.

11. Pert, *Molecules of Emotion*, 252.

12. Ibid., 257, 259. Dr. Gottesman is quoted from an interview.

13. Suryananda, "A Few Thoughts Regarding the Tantric Path."

14. Tirumular, "Tantra Seven," lines 1732–72.

15. Odier, "Shakti's Presence as Flames in the Heart."

16. Ibid.

Body Freedom Exercises
Pleasure Points

1. Gach, *Acupressure for Lovers*, 101–103, 112–114.

Dirty Dancing

2. "Don't Look Now" is available on DVD at Amazon.com: http://www.amazon.com/exec/obidos/ASIN/B000069I0A/4freedomsconsult.

3. Videos on exotic dance, how to dance for your lover, and striptease are available through the Four Freedoms website: http://www.tantra-sex.com/v-dancing.html.

Mind Freedom Exercises

Shaman Says

1. Center of Traditional Taoist Studies, "Enlightenment: Shamanism."

Posting Priorities

2. Poole, "A Bit of a Giggle." This story, widely available online in various versions, is generally attributed to Stephen Covey.

Heart Freedom Exercises

Love Potion

1. Watson, *Love Potions*, 140.

2. Ibid., 136.

Soul Freedom Exercises

The Circle

1. Morgan, *Mutant Message Down Under*, 87.

Integration Exercises

Now and Zen

1. Watson, *The Zen Teachings of Master Lin-Chi*.

Under the Sky

2. Falk, *Universe on a T-Shirt*, 151.

RECOMMENDED READING

Selected Authors

Joseph Campbell

Follow your bliss! With this as the core principle of his life's work, Campbell encouraged us all to embrace our greatness by undertaking the hero's journey and opening to the truth revealed in the myths of our lives. He died in 1987.

The Hero with a Thousand Faces
ISBN: 0-691-01784-0

This is Campbell's most important work, in which he ingeniously weaves together insights from modern psychology and ancient mythology to provide modern people with guidelines for living a full life by following bliss on the personal hero's journey. First published in 1949, this book became a bestseller in 1988 (eventually selling over a million copies) when it served as the subject for the PBS television series *The Power of Myth*. George Lucas was inspired by it in creating his *Star Wars* movies.

The Power of Myth
ISBN: 0-385-41886-8

Transcriptions of Bill Moyers interviewing Joseph Campbell for the six-part PBS television series *The Power of Myth*.

Myths to Live By
ISBN: 0-140-19461-4

In this collection of twelve essays and lectures from 1961 to 1971, Campbell explores the world's great religions from the perspective of myth rather than the traditional interpretations. Campbell describes our time as a "new age" in which "we are . . . participating in one of the very greatest leaps of the human spirit to a knowledge not only of outside nature but also of our own deep inward mystery."

Carlos Castaneda

Over eight million copies of Castaneda's books have been sold. Although critics have said his work is fiction (not ethnographically accurate), Castaneda maintained his writings were anthropology. In 1973, he was granted a Ph.D. in anthropology by the University of

California, Los Angeles (UCLA). The value of the teachings is undeniable, no matter how they are classified. By the way, his books repeatedly made the top of the bestseller lists for nonfiction books. Castaneda died in 1998. He is one of the five most important mentor authors who have influenced and guided Al's lifetime spiritual quest.

His first three books include many vivid instances of the use of hallucinatory plants to open doorways into profound experiences of nonordinary reality. Such magical encounters forced Castaneda to re-evaluate everything he thought he knew about what it means to be a man and a human being. By far the most important messages from these accounts are the lessons Don Juan patiently teaches Castaneda about being an "impeccable warrior" following a path "with heart."

In his later years, Castaneda introduced a new way to expand consciousness called Tensegrity, which includes meditations, physical movement exercises, and the integration of a body of shamanic teachings.

The Teachings of Don Juan: A Yaqui Way of Knowledge
ISBN: 0-671-60041-9

This is Castaneda's first book, introducing his long apprenticeship with the Yaqui sorcerer Don Juan Matus.

A Separate Reality: Further Conversations with Don Juan
ISBN: 0-671-73249-8

In his second book, Castaneda resumes his apprenticeship, determined to go deeper into Don Juan's world of sorcery. *A Separate Reality* is both the discovery of a hitherto unrecorded body of wisdom and knowledge and the story of a remarkable, shattering personal experience.

Journey to Ixtlan
ISBN: 0-671-73246-3

Don Juan teaches Castaneda how to see with shamanic vision to perceive things as they really are rather than merely describing them with conventional language from preconceived ideas and memories.

Ram Dass

Ram Dass, formerly Richard Alpert, was a professor dismissed from Harvard in 1963, along with colleague Timothy Leary, because of his experiments with mind-altering drugs such as LSD. In 1967, he traveled to India, found his guru (Neem Karoli Baba), and then returned to North America to share his experience of enlightenment. In 1974, Ram Dass created the Hanuman Foundation, which developed the Prison Ashram Project, designed to help prison inmates grow spiritually during their incarceration, and the Dying Project, conceived as a spiritual support structure for conscious dying. He is a cofounder and advisory board member of the Seva Foundation, an international service organization, and he also works with the Social Venture Network, an organization of businesses seeking to bring social consciousness to business practices.

Be Here Now
ISBN: 0-517-54305-2

The message in Ram Dass's first book on returning from India is profoundly simple but enormously difficult to live by: "Be here now." Where are you? Here. What time is it? Now. This book has seen over thirty-five reprints with more than one million copies sold. Reading it can change your life.

Grist for the Mill
ISBN: 0-890-87499-9

This book is full of stories that communicate what it means in daily living to "be here now." In one story, as Ram Dass is living in India following his spiritual quest, his father calls to inform him that his mother has died. He returns home wearing a robe, long hair, and beard, not looking at all like the law student his father remembers from only a year earlier. His father, one of the founders of Brandeis University and former president of the New York, New Haven & Hartford Railroad, is so embarrassed that he doesn't want his friends to see them together. How they relate to each other over the next few days, for example, in the simple act of making raspberry jam, will open your heart.

*Still Here: Embracing Aging, Changing,
and Dying*
ISBN: 1-573-22871-0

This is a book on the yoga of aging consciously. In 1997, Ram Dass experienced a stroke that left him with expressive aphasia and partial paralysis. He has learned the hard way that aging can be unkind to the body, but in every situation Dass seeks the opportunity for spiritual growth. He teaches us how to diminish our suffering despite the aches, pains, and limitations that come to us with age by stepping away from the ego-self to embrace the soul-self, where we can witness our thoughts and emotions and evaluate their effects on us. Despite the aftereffects of his stroke, Ram Dass continues a very active teaching and speaking itinerary. No one gets out of life alive. Read this book and enjoy the journey.

The Only Dance There Is
ISBN: 0-385-08413-7

This text grew out of the interaction between Ram Dass and the spiritual seekers in attendance at talks he gave at the Menninger Foundation in 1970 and at the Spring Grove Hospital in Maryland in 1972. An excellent guide for understanding the nature of consciousness, the book is full of lessons of wisdom often conveyed in the context of personal stories from his life.

Stephen Levine

Steven Levine, formerly director of the Hanuman Foundation's Dying Project, and his wife, Ondrea Levine, have been counseling the dying for over thirty years. According to Elizabeth Kübler-Ross, "His work is magic."

*Who Dies? An Investigation of Conscious Living
and Conscious Dying*
ISBN: 0-385-26221-3

The Levines provide calm compassion rather than the frightening melodrama usually surrounding death. What is the true self? What is the difference when the dying person and those around him have their hearts wide open?

*A Year to Live: How to Live This Year as If It
Were Your Last*
ISBN: 0-609-80194-5

According to Socrates, we should "always be occupied in the practice of dying" in order to be fully alive. Imagine you have one year left to live. Would this change how you live? Levine undertakes a one-year experiment to find out and shares his discoveries in this book.

Healing into Life and Death
ISBN: 0-385-26219-1

In his work with the terminally ill, Levine discovered that in preparing for death, many experienced healing, often feeling better than before they became noticeably ill. On the other hand, one of the most important insights is that healing does not always mean the patient continues to live. Often, the most profound healing took place in those who did eventually die, but their deaths were transformed into experiences of beauty and grace. Levine concluded that real healing occurred when the heart was opened and there was a balanced integration of body, mind, heart, and soul.

Meetings at the Edge: Dialogues with the Grieving and the Dying, the Healing and the Healed
ISBN: 0-385-26220-5

Levine shares the stories of the many ways people live with dying and die as an inevitable part of their life. If you are exploring how to live fully now and eventually to die with dignity, grace, and in full consciousness, this book is an excellent place to start.

John C. Lilly

The explanatory principle will save you from the fear of the unknown. I prefer the unknown . . .

John C. Lilly

In the province of the mind, there are no limits.

John C. Lilly

Lilly's list of scientific achievements requires a full page in *Who's Who in America*. He pioneered the original neuroscientific work in electrical brain stimulation, mapping out the pleasure and pain pathways in the brain. He conducted the first research on interspecies communication with dolphins and whales. He invented the isolation tank and conducted significant research on sensory deprivation. Lilly died in 2001.

Center of the Cyclone
ISBN: 0-517-52760-X

This is Lilly's map of inner space explored during his famous LSD experiments in the sensory-deprivation isolation tank that he invented. He gives detailed descriptions of various levels of consciousness on a scale including both positive and negative states. The Hollywood movie *Altered States*, directed by Ken Russell and starring William Hurt, was based on this book.

Programming the Human Biocomputer
ISBN: 1-579-51065-5

This book explores parallels between computers and the human brain. It is Lilly's attempt to write an owner's operating manual on how to use the brain and central nervous system.

Franklin Merrell-Wolff

Franklin Merrell-Wolff (mystic, author, philosopher, mathematician) grounds his philosophy and teaching not in rational speculation but in personal, direct, mystical realizations. Wolff's spiritual search drew him to the philosophical works of the Indian sage Shankara, founder of the Advaita Vedanta school of Hindu philosophy. The following two books provide a detailed record of his realizations and a lucid philosophical description of Transcendental Consciousness. Wolff died in 1985.

Pathways through to Space
ISBN: 0-517-52777-4

This is the story of Wolff's personal realization of nirvana—God Consciousness.

The Philosophy of Consciousness Without an Object: Reflections on the Nature of Transcendental Consciousness
ISBN: 0-517-54949-2

This is the author's philosophy of Transcendental Consciousness based upon his realization of nirvana. The fundamental principle in all of Wolff's teaching is that consciousness is primary (original) and not derived from anything else.

Alan Watts

For more than forty years, Alan Watts earned a reputation as the most authoritative and insightful interpreter of Eastern philosophies for Western readers. Watts has such a unique way with words that you might feel as if you were reading your own thoughts. Author of more than twenty-five books (every one a gem to read), he was an editor, Anglican priest, graduate dean, broadcaster, lecturer, and entertainer. He held fellowships from Harvard University and the Bollinger Foundation and was Episcopal chaplain at Northwestern University during World War II. He became professor and dean of the American Academy of Asian Studies in San Francisco, created the series "Eastern Wisdom and Modern Life" for National Educational Television, and served as a visiting consultant for psychiatric institutions, hospitals, and the United States Air Force. He traveled widely, including such countries as Japan, Burma, Ceylon, and India. Watts died in 1973.

Tao: The Watercourse Way
ISBN: 0-394-73311-8

This was Watts's last book and is the one many consider his finest. Written beautifully and eloquently, it is a work of both scholarship and poetry. The depth of clarity in spiritual wisdom is remarkable.

Behold the Spirit: A Study in the Necessity of Mystical Religion
ISBN: 0-394-71761-9

This book explores how traditional Western religious doctrine can be reconciled with the intuitive religion of the Orient.

Buddhism: The Religion of No-Religion; The Edited Transcripts
ISBN: 0-804-83203-X

This is a collection of Watts's recorded lectures, in which he lays bare with lucid description the most difficult Buddhist concepts.

Nature, Man and Woman
ISBN: 0-679-73233-0

This book re-examines humanity's place in the natural world and the spirit's relation to the flesh in the light of Chinese Taoism.

Psychotherapy East and West
ISBN: 0-394-71609-4

In this book, Watts explores the common ground between Western psychiatry and Eastern philosophy in realizing the self-actualizing goals of freedom, self-expression, and authenticity.

The Way of Zen
ISBN: 0-375-70510-4

Along with D. T. Suzuki, Alan Watts was one of the first authors to introduce Zen into North America. This book, first published in 1957, is divided into two sections: history and practice. Topics include the philosophical foundations of Zen in Hinduism, the development of the early Mahayana school of Buddhism, the birth of Zen from Buddhism's marriage with Chinese Taoism, and Zen in Japan.

The Wisdom of Insecurity
ISBN: 0-394-70468-1

This is Watts's exploration of man's quest for psychological security and spiritual certainty through religion and philosophy. Watts wrote this book just after leaving the Episcopal Church because of the disturbing realization that he couldn't reconcile official theology and his duties as a priest with his personal Eastern view of reality.

This Is It, and Other Essays on Zen and Spiritual Experience
ISBN: 0-394-71904-2

The six essays in this volume all deal with the relationship of mystical experience to ordinary life. The title essay on "cosmic consciousness" includes the author's account of his own ventures into this inward realm. "Instinct, Intelligence, and Anxiety" is a study of the paradoxes of self-consciousness; "Spiritually and Sensuality," a lively discussion of the false opposition of spirit and matter; and "The New Alchemy," a balanced account of states of consciousness akin to spiritual experience induced with the aid of LSD. The collection also includes the text of Watts's celebrated pamphlet "Beat Zen, Square Zen, and Zen."

Selected Topics

Breathing

Dennis Lewis, *Free Your Breath, Free Your Life: How Conscious Breathing Can Relieve Stress, Increase Vitality, and Help You Live More Fully*
ISBN: 1-590-30133-1

Lewis demonstrates how to find the breathing practices most suitable to you rather than assuming there is one best way to breathe for everyone. Choose from seven different self-directed ways of working with breath. Want to reduce the stress load in your life? Breathing properly is one of the best places to start.

Dennis Lewis, *The Tao of Natural Breathing: For Health, Well-Being and Inner Growth*
ISBN: 0-965-16110-2

This book is an excellent guide on breathing for vitality, health, and spiritual awakening. It has been translated and published in numerous languages.

Buddhism

Stephen Batchelor, *Buddhism Without Beliefs: A Contemporary Guide to Awakening*
ISBN: 1-573-22656-4

According to this former Buddhist monk, you don't need to believe anything in order to apply the practices of Buddhism, such as mindfulness. Much of it comes down to being fully awake and present from moment to moment.

Bhante Henepola Gunaratana, *Eight Mindful Steps to Happiness: Walking the Buddha's Path*
ISBN: 0-861-71176-9

Happiness is a skill. According to Gunaratana (a Buddhist monk from Sri Lanka), "The present moment is your teacher." The eight steps to happiness (the Buddhist noble eight-fold path) are: skillful understanding, skillful thinking, skillful speech, skillful action, skill-ful livelihood, skillful effort, skillful mindful-ness, and skillful concentration.

Bhante Henepola Gunaratana, *Mindfulness in Plain English*
ISBN: 0-861-71321-4

This book is a Theravadan Buddhist medita-tion manual emphasizing Vipassana (insight) meditation. Theravada means "Doctrine of the Elders." Gunaratana emphasizes that mind-fulness is the key to waking up. Excellent for beginners. Learn it quickly, master it over a lifetime.

Steve Hagen, *Buddhism Plain and Simple*
ISBN: 0-767-90332-3

According to Hagen, Buddhism "is . . . about awareness. Not awareness of something in particular, but awareness itself, being awake, alert, in touch with what is actually happen-ing. It's about examining and exploring the most basic questions of life. It's about relying on the immediate experience of this present moment. It's about freedom of mind."

Thich Nhat Hanh, *Heart of Buddha's Teaching*
ISBN: 0-767-90369-2

Thich Nhat Hanh's skill as a poet is apparent in this excellent introduction to Buddhism. All of Hanh's writing emphasizes mindfulness—being fully present in the now moment.

The Dalai Lama and Jeffrey Hopkins,
How to Practice: The Way to a Meaningful Life
ISBN: 0-743-42708-4

The Dalai Lama teaches how to make every action part of your spiritual practice and, in doing so, create a meaningful life filled with happiness. He recommends disconnecting the attachment of your happiness from the material circumstances of your life and open-ing instead to the true source of your hap-piness, which is your inner peace of mind. There is a section on Buddhist Tantra and a discussion of how sexuality can be used in the search for peace and kindness. *Dalai Lama* means "ocean of wisdom." The fourteenth Dalai Lama (Tenzin Gyatso) won the Nobel Peace Prize in 1989 as the exiled spiritual leader of Tibet. At the age of two, in accor-dance with Tibetan tradition, he was recog-nized as the reincarnation of his predecessor, the thirteenth Dalai Lama. In 1950 (the year of the Chinese invasion of Tibet), at age six-teen, he was called upon to assume full politi-cal power and leadership. Since 1960, he has resided in Dharamsala, India, aptly known as "Little Lhasa," the seat of the Tibetan govern-ment in exile.

Sharon Salzberg, *Lovingkindness: The Revolutionary Art of Happiness*
ISBN: 1-570-62176-4

Salzberg is founder of the Insight Meditation Society in Massachusetts. Her loving-kind-ness (compassion) meditations are designed to help you realize deeper connections of in-timacy with others and peace of mind within. She encourages you not just to think about loving kindness but to take action.

Zen Buddhism

Eugen Herrigel, *Zen in the Art of Archery*
ISBN: 0-375-70509-0

There is the Zen of no mind, in which you eat when hungry, rest when tired, and stop when finished. There is also the Zen known through the ritualized arts of discipline and beauty, such as archery, swordsmanship, brush-and-ink, the tea ceremony, or flower arranging. This book is Herrigel's story of striking the target bull's-eye blindfolded.

Robert M. Pirsig, *Zen and the Art of Motorcycle Maintenance: An Inquiry into Values*
ISBN: 0-060-95832-4

This is a book suitable for the deepest thinker while at the same time opening the heart. It is worthy to be read many times. One of the best books Al has ever read.

Paul Reps, *Zen Flesh, Zen Bones*
ISBN: 1-570-62063-6

No preachy doctrine here, just a simple collection of 101 stories, carefully chosen and gracefully translated, that leave the reader in a state of wonder, curiosity, and puzzlement. Many of these stories have seeped into the culture of North America, and you will likely recognize some of them, such as the story of the Zen master overflowing a visiting professor's tea cup to illustrate how filled the professor is with himself—so filled he cannot learn anything new.

Philip Kapleau Roshi, *The Three Pillars of Zen: Teaching, Practice, and Enlightenment*
ISBN: 0-385-26093-8

Roshi is a Zen master who writes from personal experience, beginning with his time in Japan during the 1950s. This book has been reprinted in thirty-five editions, and many consider it the best book on Zen ever written.

D. T. Suzuki, *An Introduction to Zen Buddhism*
ISBN: 0-802-13055-0

D. T. Suzuki (1870–1966), long considered the foremost Western authority on Zen Buddhism, is usually credited with introducing the subject to America. He was a professor of Buddhist studies (not a Zen adept himself), so this book, based on articles written in Japan in 1914, is a scholarly report rather than one of personal experience.

Taoism

John Blofeld, *Taoism*
ISBN: 1-570-62589-1

"From the Tao all the myriad objects derive their being, their illusory separateness being wrought by the interplay of yin and yang." Blofeld has published many books on Buddhism, Taoism, and Tantra.

Thomas Cleary, *Practical Taoism*
ISBN: 1-570-62200-0

Cleary, a well-known translator of books on oriental philosophy and practice, here simplifies Taoist concepts, hence the use of the term "practical" in the title. Sometimes the simplest is the most profound.

Thomas Cleary, *The Taoist Classics: The Collected Translations of Thomas Cleary*, Vol. 2, *Understanding Reality; The Inner Teachings of Taoism; The Book of Balance and Harmony; Practical Taoism*
ISBN: 1-570-62486-0

This is a more rigorous academic treatment of this complex topic. Over the past twenty years, Cleary has translated more than fifty Buddhist, Taoist, and Confucian texts. He has a Ph.D. in East Asian Languages and Literature from Harvard but is not affiliated with any university.

Eva Wong, *The Shambhala Guide to Taoism*
ISBN: 1-570-62169-1

This book is divided into three sections: history of Taoism, systems of Taoism, and Taoist practices. It explores the many varieties of Taoist practice and includes an extensive suggested reading list.

Taoist Sacred Sexuality— Mantak Chia

Healing Love through the Tao: Cultivating Female Sexual Energy
ISBN: 0-935-62105-9

Taoist Secrets of Love: Cultivating Male Sexual Energy
ISBN: 0-943-35819-1

Mantak Chia is a master who gives detailed descriptions of the how-to of moving sexual energy. The methods he proposes are very disciplined and therefore work best for people who like structure and have lots of patience and self-motivation. These books are also good for individuals not in a relationship, because so much of the work is done on one's own. Because Chia's work derives from the Taoist tradition (as opposed to Tantric), there is more emphasis on the physical and practical than the mystical and emotional aspects of the work. These are two of the most important books that Pala and Al used in cutting their teeth on sacred sexuality.

The Multi-Orgasmic Woman: Discover Your Full Desire, Pleasure, and Vitality
ISBN: 1-594-86027-0

This book explores how women can adopt a pleasure orientation with sex rather than seeking orgasm as a goal of lovemaking. Nevertheless, it offers a step-by-step guide for women in becoming multi-orgasmic.

The Multi-Orgasmic Man: Sexual Secrets Every Man Should Know
ISBN: 0-062-51336-2

This book is an excellent step-by-step, how-to manual for achieving sexual ecstasy. In spite of the title, this book is for women as well as men.

The Multi-Orgasmic Couple
ISBN: 0-062-51614-0

Discover how to have multiple whole-body orgasms and how to reach ever more fulfilling levels of intimacy and ecstasy together.

Tantra

Daniel Cozort, *Highest Yoga Tantra*
ISBN: 1-559-39036-0

Explores the Tantric practices of generation and completion meditations leading to enlightenment. Emptiness and bliss are two main themes in the book.

Shri Dharmakirti, *Mahayana Tantra: An Introduction*
ISBN: 0-143-02853-7

Shri Dharmakirti, practitioner of Mahayana Buddhist Tantra, is a disciple of the current Dalai Lama. He received initiations and instructions in the practice of highest secret mantra and was inducted into the lineage of Lama Tsongkhapa.

Georg Feuerstein, *Tantra: Path of Ecstasy*
ISBN: 1-570-62304-X

Feuerstein's work, drawn from Hindu sources, deals with the nonsexual aspects of Tantric practice. In this book, he has assembled an important selection of Hindu, Tantric, and Shaivite texts difficult to find elsewhere.

Kelsang Gyatso Geshe, *Guide to Dakini Land: The Highest Yoga Tantra Practice of Buddha Vajrayogini*
ISBN: 0-948-00639-0

A thorough explanation of the Tantric practice of Vajrayogini, the female Buddha of wisdom, this text provides detailed instructions on the eleven yogas of the generation stage and an explanation of the essential completion stage practices leading to enlightenment. Also included are methods for transforming ordinary daily activities into spiritual meditations.

Bhagwan Shree Rajneesh, *Tantra, the Supreme Understanding: Discourses on the Tantric Way of Tilopa's Song of Mahamudra*
ISBN: 0-880-50643-1

Unlike most Tantra authors, Bhagwan Rajneesh, also known as Osho, was undeniably a great Tantric master. This fact lends significant weight to his many publications on Tantra and sacred sexuality.

Swami Satyananda Saraswati, *Kundalini Tantra*
ISBN: 8-185-78715-8

Swami Satyananda Saraswati founded the International Yoga Fellowship in 1963 and the Bihar School of Yoga in 1964. This text explores practices to awaken the kundalini energy.

Swami Satyananda Saraswati, *Meditations from the Tantras*
ISBN: 8-185-78711-5

This book helps readers turn every action of life into an act of sadhana (spiritual practice) by using meditation techniques that have their origin in Tantra.

Pandit Rajmani Tigunait, *Sakti: The Power in Tantra; A Scholarly Approach*
ISBN: 0-893-89154-1

This book clarifies how Tantric philosophy and practice unify the concepts of yantra, mandala, mantra, chakra, kundalini, deities, and ritualistic and meditative practices. It explains the relationship among the different branches of Tantra, including an exploration of some of the controversy concerning the differences between right-hand (nonsexual) and left-hand (sexual) Tantric practices.

The Dalai Lama, Tsong-Ka-Pa, and Jeffrey Hopkins, *Deity Yoga: In Action and Performance Tantras*
ISBN: 0-937-93850-5

Teaches the meditative techniques of Action and Performance Tantras.

The Dalai Lama, Tsong-Ka-Pa, and Jeffrey Hopkins, *Tantra in Tibet*
ISBN: 0-937-93849-1

Excellent discussion of the Tantric doctrine of emptiness.

Wei Wu Wei, *Why Lazarus Laughed: The Essential Doctrine; Zen—Advaita—Tantra*
ISBN: 1-591-81011-6

Wei Wu Wei, who has become an underground cult figure, explores the essential doctrine shared by the traditions of Zen Buddhism, Advaita Vedanta, and Tantra. Born in Ireland in 1895 and raised in England, he attended Oxford and then traveled extensively throughout Asia, spending some time at the ashram of Sri Ramana Maharshi. He published eight books before his death in 1986 at age ninety.

David Gordon White, ed., *Tantra in Practice*
ISBN: 0-691-05778-8

This book includes plays, transcribed interviews, poetry, parodies, inscriptions, instructional texts, scriptures, philosophical conjectures, dreams, and astronomical speculations. There are thirty-six texts from China, India, Japan, Nepal, and Tibet, ranging from the seventh century to the present day.

Lama Yeshe, Philip Glass, and Jonathan Landaw, ed., *Introduction to Tantra: The Transformation of Desire*
ISBN: 0-861-71162-9

This is primarily a nonsexual exploration of Tantra. Al particularly liked the section on the subject of death and after death.

Tantra—Daniel Odier

Daniel Odier, who has taught Eastern spiritual traditions at a number of American universities, founded the Tantra/Chan (Zen) Center in Paris. In addition to his books on Tantra, he has also published a number of mystery novels, one of which was made into an award-winning film, *Devi the Goddess*. His novels are published under the pseudonym of Delacorta. Of all the Tantra books Al has read over the past twenty years, Odier's *Desire* and *Tantric Quest* are his top two choices.

Desire: The Tantric Path to Awakening
ISBN: 0-892-81858-1

According to almost all of the great world religions, including Buddhism, desire is an enemy blocking the path to enlightenment. Contrary to this, Daniel Odier maintains that desire is the only true path to liberation. According to Odier, the primary requirement for a spiritual seeker to fully awaken

is simple, direct, personal experience. He refers to his disciplined approach as "micro-practices" involving the conscious withdrawal from habitual activities for just a few seconds several times a day. There is no goal in this practice, no seeking to get somewhere or accomplish something, but rather the purpose is simply to be fully aware, fully awake, and fully present to your own divinity in the now moment. Odier describes his Tantric path as "nothing spectacular . . . lack[ing] in the exotic, the magickal, the extraordinary. . . . There was no ritual other than to breathe, walk, bathe . . . to look at the earth, the lichens, the trees, the leaves, common objects; to enter deeply into contact with life, reality." He suggests that the "luminosity of existence" pervades everything, including you. Odier received direct personal Tantric initiation from a Kashmiri Shaivite yogini, Lalita Devi, in the Tantric lineage of the Tibetan master Kalu Rinpoche, which dates back several thousand years.

Yoga Spandakarika: The Sacred Texts at the Origins of Tantra
ISBN: 1-594-77051-4

This book presents translations of early Tantras (sacred Tantric texts).

Tantric Quest: An Encounter with Absolute Love
ISBN: 0-892-81620-1

In this story of his personal spiritual quest to find a Tantric master, Odier wanders through India, where an unusual, sometimes disastrous, sequence of events leads him deep in the forest to yogini Lalita Devi. Over a period of months, Odier undergoes a series of trials, tests, and rituals of purification that culminate in a sacred sex initiation in which he experiences the awakening of the kundalini and the joining of the divine forces of Shiva and Shakti.

Nirvana Tao: The Secret Meditation Techniques of the Taoist and Buddhist Masters
ISBN: 0-892-81045-9

Odier's teaching emphasizes direct personal experience to reach enlightenment using visualization and meditation. Here he reveals secret spiritual practices of masters with whom he studied at Buddhist and Taoist monasteries throughout India, Nepal, Sri Lanka, Thailand, and Japan.

Tantric Sacred Sexuality

Pala Copeland and Al Link, *Soul Sex: Tantra for Two*
ISBN: 1-564-14664-2

Our first book explores relationship as spiritual practice, using Tantric and Taoist approaches to sacred sexuality. We help you learn how to create love for a lifetime together.

Margo Anand, *The Art of Sexual Ecstasy: The Path of Sacred Sexuality for Western Lovers*
ISBN: 0-874-77581-7

This book is a complete sacred sex course in itself. With lots of meditations, activities, and exercises, it is particularly suited for couples who want to open up to each other emotionally as well as physically.

Nik Douglas and Penny Slinger,
Sexual Secrets: The Alchemy of Ecstasy
ISBN: 0-892-81805-0

First published in 1979, this popular book (over one million copies sold) presents a concise and articulate overview of the history and philosophy of sacred sex. Practical exercises and meditations are interspersed throughout. It will work well for people who like to know the background of what they are doing and would like to pick and choose and create on their own the activities they will do in their exploration. It overflows with wonderful erotic drawings by Penny Slinger.

Julie Henderson, *The Lover Within: Opening to Energy in Sexual Practice*
ISBN: 1-581-77017-0

This book is an excellent how-to manual for working with your sexual energy. It might alter both how you think about love and sex and what you do in intimate practice. The focus is on neither manipulative technique nor personal history but on the process of energy itself. It provides exercises to be experienced alone or with a partner and offers instruction on how to move, collect, heighten, and share energy.

Diana Richardson, *Tantric Orgasm for Women*
ISBN: 0-892-81133-1

Excellent presentation of information about the polarity of the different chakras and the role of breasts in the female orgasmic response. The best discussion we have seen of the experience of a valley orgasm. She explains how to relax into a whole-body orgasm rather than achieving it as a goal.

Ma Ananda Sarita and Swami Anand Geho, *Ecstatic Sex: A Guide to the Pleasures of Tantra*
ISBN: 0-743-24610-1

This text explores Tantric sexuality, including basic sexual anatomy, opening your chakras, self-pleasuring, foreplay, creative positions, and orgasm. Ma Ananda Sarita and Swami Anand Geho have taught Tantra at Osho Multiversity in India.

Ma Ananda Sarita and Swami Anand Geho, *Tantric Love: A Nine-Step Guide to Transforming Lovers into Soul Mates*
ISBN: 0-743-21531-1

This book illustrates ways couples can open to a deeper intimacy. Each chapter focuses on one of the chakras (the body's energy centers) and offers simple exercises to help you share this energy, opening the door to ecstasy.

Vedanta

All styles of yoga are part of the Indian Hindu Vedanta spiritual tradition, and they are all undertaken with the purpose (not goal) of awakening to full self-realization, enlightenment, nirvana, or God Consciousness. These terms are used here interchangeably, all suggesting the same outcome, to allow the ego-self to dissolve into union with absolute consciousness. There are many types of yoga, and each of these categories contains many variations.

Some of the most important schools of yoga:

- Bhakti yoga is the path of pure love or devotion to God.

- Karma yoga is the path of selfless action, with all activities and results offered to God.

- Raja yoga (Royal yoga) is an eightfold path teaching how to use the mind to approach union with God.

- Jnana yoga is the path of knowledge leading to the ability to discriminate between the real and illusion, leading to liberation or enlightenment.

- Tantra yoga is the path of transforming sexual energy into spiritual energy, leading to nirvana or God Consciousness.

- Kundalini yoga is the path of awakening the kundalini energy at the base of the spine. As it moves up through the body, opening all the chakras, there is an experience of enlightenment.

- Hatha yoga is the path of using physical body movement (asanas) and breathing (pranayama) for the purpose of self-realization.

Paul Deussen and A. S. Geden, trans., *The Philosophy of the Upanishads*
ISBN: 8-120-81620-X

Paul Deussen, a student roommate of Friedrich Nietzsche and a professor of Sanskrit at the University of Kiel in Germany, dedicated thirty-five years of his life to the study of Indian philosophy. Originally published in German (*Die Philosophie der Upanishads*) a century ago, this book was translated into English by A. S. Geden in 1906. According to Deussen, the philosophy of the Upanishads is the "culminating point of the Indian doctrine of the universe" and "in philosophical significance has been surpassed by none of the later developments of thought up to the present day."

Eliot Deutsch, *Advaita Vedanta: A Philosophical Reconstruction*
ISBN: 0-824-80271-3

Deutsch, former editor of the prestigious journal *Philosophy East and West*, is a professor of philosophy at the University of Hawaii. This short book admirably distills the essence of Advaita Vedanta, the system of nondualistic thought and philosophy presented by Shankara (ca. 788–820) in which all boundaries and distinctions are unreal, reality is not made up of parts, and "in essence it is not different from the Self." There is only the Self, Brahman, or the One, a state "which is ultimately a name for the timeless plenitude of being."

Christopher Isherwood, *Vedanta for the Western World*
ISBN: 0-874-81000-0

Isherwood, a well-known novelist and playwright, became a follower of Swami Prabhavananda (an Indian monk of the Ramakrishna order) in 1943, after which he authored several books on Indian Vedanta. This book, first published in 1944, presents a collection of essays comparing the principles of Hinduism, Buddhism, and Christianity.

Christopher Isherwood and Swami Prabhavananda, trans., *Bhagavad-Gita: The Song of God*
ISBN: 0-451-52844-1

The *Bhagavad-Gita* (written between the fifth and second centuries BCE) is the gospel of Hinduism, and one of the great religious classics of the world. It is the story of a battlefield conversation between the warrior-prince Arjuna and Lord Krishna. Krishna explains the nature of the soul and the various types of yoga, or paths to God. Arjuna is extremely distressed at the prospect of having to kill his own relatives in the pending battle. Krishna explains that souls can never die and that Arjuna must play his assigned role in the great scheme of things. Krishna teaches Arjuna how to balance the spiritual journey with worldly obligations.

Christopher Isherwood and Swami Prabhavananda, trans., *How to Know God: The Yoga Aphorisms of Patanjali*
ISBN: 0-874-81041-8

Patanjali's Sutras are dated sometime between the fourth century BCE and the fourth century CE. The teachings offer methods for creating a direct personal experience of God Consciousness, "the Reality which underlies this apparent, ephemeral universe." According to the text, in order to know God, one must first cease identifying with the mind. Then it is possible to know God everywhere, "both within and without, instantly present and infinitely elsewhere, the dweller in the atom and the abode of all things."

Swami B. V. Tripurari, *Aesthetic Vedanta: The Sacred Path of Passionate Love*
ISBN: 1-886-06914-X

An elegant masterpiece of prose, philosophy, and translation, this book presents a timeless story of erotic, spiritual, and romantic love in a translation of the Sanskrit poem "Rasalila," the sacred love affair of Radha and Krishna.

Yoga

Yoga means "union." Although many in the West automatically assume that yoga means Hatha yoga and that it is primarily for physical fitness and health, the purpose of all yoga is to enable the practitioner to realize wholeness by reuniting body, mind, heart, and soul, ultimately awakening to enlightenment. Hatha yoga is a physical, energetic, and spiritual practice suitable to any age, health status, or fitness level. Most styles of Hatha yoga emphasize relaxing into the physical movements rather than straining to go further than your body is comfortable with. Generally speaking, don't bother with yoga unless you intend to slow down. One exception is Astanga yoga, a vigorous workout quite suitable for training athletes.

Beryl Bender Birch, *Power Yoga: The Total Strength and Flexibility Workout*
ISBN: 0-020-58351-6

Astanga yoga is an active form of Hatha yoga designed to build fitness, strength, flexibility, and endurance for athletes.

Laurent de Brunhoff, *Babar's Yoga for Elephants*
ISBN: 0-810-91021-7

Get this for your kids. Get them started with yoga now. Obesity in children is becoming an epidemic. Clear, easy, simple, fun. As Babar explains, yoga "helps us all to relax and draw strength from our inner elephant." Watercolor illustrations by Brunhoff.

H. David Coulter, *Anatomy of Hatha Yoga: A Manual for Students, Teachers, and Practitioners*
ISBN: 0-970-70060-1

Coulter's Ph.D. is in anatomy. His book presents an authoritative correlation between the practices of Hatha yoga (asanas, breathing, relaxation, meditation) and physiology. Featuring 230 black-and-white photographs and more than 120 diagrams and anatomical illustrations, this book won the 2002 Benjamin Franklin Award for Health, Wellness, and Nutrition from the Publishers Marketing Association.

T. K. V. Desikachar and R. H. Cravens, *Health, Healing and Beyond: Yoga and the Living Tradition of Krishnamacharya*
ISBN: 0-893-81731-7

According to some authorities, Krishnamacharya, who lived for more than one hundred years, is the source for nearly all modern yoga practices. Written by his son Desikachar, this book is a biographical profile of Krishnamacharya's life and work. Tirumalai Krishnamacharya (1888–1989), considered a saint by some, was a guru to thousands. His guiding principle as a teacher was, "Teach what is inside you." In the 1930s, American and European medical experts reported the yogi's astonishing ability to stop both his heartbeat and his breath, essentially to control the life process itself.

Georg Feuerstein, *The Yoga Tradition: Its History, Literature, Philosophy and Practice*
ISBN: 1-890-77218-6

In this scholarly exploration of yoga, Feuerstein, author of more than two dozen books on yoga, presents a substantial overview of yogic traditions and styles, in terms of history, philosophy, literature, psychology, and practice. Included also are the translations of twenty classic yoga texts.

Suza Francina, *The New Yoga for People Over 50: A Comprehensive Guide for Midlife and Older Beginners*
ISBN: 1-558-74453-3

It's never too late to start your practice of yoga. Yoga is widely credited with slowing down and even reversing the aging process. This book presents the Iyengar style of Hatha yoga with asanas (postures) specially adapted for people between fifty and seventy years old. For example, the author shows how to use chairs, walls, wall ropes, bolsters, back-bending benches, and straps to aid in the exercises. Illustrated with over a hundred easy-to-follow instructional photos.

Sharon Gannon and David Life, *Jivamukti Yoga: Practices for Liberating Body and Soul*
ISBN: 0-345-44208-3

The word *jivamukti* refers to a liberated or enlightened being. This book presents the Vinyassa style of Hatha yoga, sometimes referred to as "flow" yoga because the postures smoothly flow into one another. It emphasizes the integration of breathing, movement, and postures. Like Astanga yoga, this approach is much more vigorous than regular Hatha yoga.

Richard Hittleman, *Richard Hittleman's Yoga: 28 Day Exercise Plan*
ISBN: 0-911-10421-6

Illustrated with over five hundred photographs, Hittleman's book tells you exactly what to do each day. In twenty-eight days, you will be physically renewed.

B. K. S. Iyengar and Yehudi Menuhin, *Light on Yoga: The Bible of Modern Yoga*
ISBN: 0-805-21031-8

Considered by many authorities to be the definitive book on Hatha yoga and used as a reference text by innumerable professional yoga teachers, *Light on Yoga* details step-by-step instructions for the selected asanas (postures) and three important pranayam (breathing) exercises. The book includes over six hundred photos of Iyengar demonstrating the practices.

John McAfee, *The Secret of the Yamas: A Spiritual Guide to Yoga*
ISBN: 0-971-15690-5

John McAfee is the founder of the Relational Yoga Mandiram in Woodland Park, Colorado, and organizer of the annual Sidha Silence retreats in the Rocky Mountains. This book presents the relationship between yoga asanas (physical postures) and the yogic philosophy of Pantanjali, who is widely credited with first documenting the practice and philosophy of yoga over two thousand years ago. The author explores the integration of yogic practice with an open heart and clear mind. According to McAfee, the source of all problems, as well as the answers, lies within each of us. Yamas provide guidelines to changing our behaviors as we take responsibility for what we are creating in our lives.

Erich Schiffmann, *Yoga: The Spirit and Practice of Moving into Stillness*
ISBN: 0-671-53480-7

An excellent exploration of Hatha yoga, this book supplies detailed descriptions of the asana physical postures, explanations of how they affect the physical and energetic (qi or prana) bodies, and details about breathing, relaxation, and meditation. Schiffman is schooled in the Iyengar and Desikachar approaches to yoga.

WORKS CONSULTED

American Society for Aesthetic Plastic Surgery (ASAPS). "Cosmetic Surgery Quick Facts: 2005 ASAPS Statistics." ASAPS Press Center. http://www.surgery.org/press/procedurefacts-asqf.php.

Anand, Margo. *The Art of Sexual Ecstasy: The Path of Sacred Sexuality for Western Lovers.* New York: Jeremy P. Tarcher, 1991.

Armstrong, Rebecca. "Joseph Campbell Foundation Myth Letter." Joseph Campbell Foundation (November 2001). http://www.jcf.org/myth_letter.php?mid=9.

Batchelor, Stephen. *Buddhism Without Beliefs: A Contemporary Guide to Awakening.* New York: Riverhead Books, 1998.

Birch, Beryl Bender. *Power Yoga: The Total Strength and Flexibility Workout.* New York: Fireside, 1995.

Blanchflower, David G., and Andrew J. Oswald. "Money, Sex and Happiness: An Empirical Study." NBER Working Paper No. 10499. National Bureau of Economic Research (May 2004). http://www.nber.org/papers/W10499. Cited in: Kirchheimer, Sid. "Sex Better Than Money for Happiness." *WebMD Medical News* (July 16, 2004). http://my.webmd.com/content/Article/90/100853.htm.

Blofeld, John. *Taoism.* Boston: Shambhala, 2000.

Bloom, Howard. "The History of the Global Brain: Interspecies Global Mind XX." Telepolis (August 12, 1999). http://www.heise.de/tp/english/special/glob/6556/1.html.

Blum, Deborah. *Sex on the Brain: The Biological Differences Between Men and Women.* New York: Viking, 1997.

Brunhoff, Laurent de. *Babar's Yoga for Elephants.* New York: Harry N. Abrams, 2002.

Campbell, Joseph. *The Hero's Journey.* Edited by Phil Cousineau. Novato, CA: New World Library, 2003.

———. *The Hero with a Thousand Faces.* Princeton, NJ: Princeton University Press, 1972.

———. *Myths to Live By.* New York: Penguin, 1993.

Campbell, Joseph, and Bill Moyers. *The Power of Myth.* Edited by Betty Sue Flowers. New York: Anchor Books, 1991.

Carse, James P. *Finite and Infinite Games.* New York: Ballantine Books, 1994.

Castaneda, Carlos. *Journey to Ixtlan.* New York: Washington Square Press, 1991.

———. *A Separate Reality: Further Conversations with Don Juan*. New York: Washington Square Press, 1991.

———. *The Teachings of Don Juan: A Yaqui Way of Knowledge*. New York: Washington Square Press, 1985.

Center of Traditional Taoist Studies. "Enlightenment: Shamanism." TAO.org. https://maxvps001.maximumasp.com/v001u23zac/Tao/Enlightenment/Magic/Shamanism.asp (registration required).

Chia, Mantak. *Taoist Secrets of Love: Cultivating Male Sexual Energy*. Santa Fe, NM: Aurora Press, 1984.

Chia, Mantak, and Rachel Carlton Abrams. *The Multi-Orgasmic Woman: Discover Your Full Desire, Pleasure, and Vitality*. Emmaus, PA: Rodale Books, 2005.

Chia, Mantak, and Douglas Abrams Arava. *The Multi-Orgasmic Man: Sexual Secrets Every Man Should Know*. San Francisco: HarperSanFrancisco, 1997.

Chia, Mantak, and Maneewan Chia. *Healing Love through the Tao: Cultivating Female Sexual Energy*. Huntington, NY: Healing Tao Books, 1991.

Chia, Mantak, Maneewan Chia, and Douglas Abrams Arava. *The Multi-Orgasmic Couple*. San Francisco: HarperSanFrancisco, 2002.

Cleary, Thomas. *Practical Taoism*. Boston: Shambhala, 1996.

———. *The Taoist Classics: The Collected Translations of Thomas Cleary*. Vol. 2, *Understanding Reality; The Inner Teachings of Taoism; The Book of Balance and Harmony; Practical Taoism*. Boston: Shambhala, 1999.

Copeland, Pala, and Al Link. *Soul Sex: Tantra for Two*. Franklin Lakes, NJ: New Page Books, 2003.

Corn, Laura. *101 Nights of Grrreat Romance: How to Make Love with Your Clothes On*. Oklahoma City, OK: Park Avenue Publishers, 1996.

———. *101 Nights of Grrreat Sex: Secret Sealed Seductions for Fun-Loving Couples*. Oklahoma City, OK: Park Avenue Publishers, 2000.

Coulter, H. David. *Anatomy of Hatha Yoga: A Manual for Students, Teachers, and Practitioners*. Honesdale, PA: Body and Breath, 2001.

Cozort, Daniel. *Highest Yoga Tantra*. Ithaca, NY: Snow Lion Publications, 1994.

Dalai Lama XIV, and Jeffrey Hopkins. *How to Practice: The Way to a Meaningful Life*. New York: Atria, 2002.

Dalai Lama XIV, Tsong-Ka-Pa, and Jeffrey Hopkins. *Deity Yoga: In Action and Performance Tantras*. Ithaca, NY: Snow Lion Publications, 1987.

———. *Tantra in Tibet*. Ithaca, NY: Snow Lion Publications, 1987.

Dass, Ram. *Be Here Now*. New York: Three Rivers Press, 1971.

———. *Grist for the Mill*. Berkeley, CA: Celestial Arts, 1988.

———. *The Only Dance There Is*. New York: Anchor Books, 1974.

———. *Still Here: Embracing Aging, Changing, and Dying*. New York: Riverhead Books, 2001.

Desikachar, T. K. V., and R. H. Cravens. *Health, Healing and Beyond: Yoga and the Living Tradition of Krishnamacharya*. New York: Aperture, 1998.

Deussen, Paul, and A. S. Geden, trans. *The Philosophy of the Upanishads*. Delhi: Motilal Banarsidass, 1999.

Deutsch, Eliot. *Advaita Vedanta: A Philosophical Reconstruction*. Honolulu: University of Hawaii Press, 1969.

Dharmakirti, Shri. *Mahayana Tantra: An Introduction*. New York: Penguin, 2002.

Donnelly, Denise, Elisabeth Burgess, Sally Anderson, Regina Davis, and Joy Dillard. "Involuntary Celibacy: A Life Course Analysis." *Journal of Sex Research* (May 2001): 159. Cited in: Kirchheimer, Sid. "Sex Better Than Money for Happiness." *WebMD Medical News* (July 16, 2004). http://my.webmd.com/content/Article/90/100853.htm.

Douglas, Nik, and Penny Slinger. *Sexual Secrets: The Alchemy of Ecstasy*. Rochester, VT: Inner Traditions, 1999.

Emerson, Ralph Waldo. "The Over-Soul." *Essays: First Series* (1841). RWE.org: The Works of Ralph Waldo Emerson. http://rwe.org/works/Essays-1st_Series_09_The_Over-Soul.htm.

Falk, Dan. *Universe on a T-Shirt: The Quest for the Theory of Everything*. Toronto: Viking Canada, 2002.

Feuerstein, Georg. *Tantra: Path of Ecstasy*. Boston: Shambhala, 1998.

———. *The Yoga Tradition: Its History, Literature, Philosophy and Practice*. Prescott, AZ: Hohm Press, 2001.

Francina, Suza. *The New Yoga for People Over 50: A Comprehensive Guide for Midlife and Older Beginners*. Deerfield Beach, FL: Health Communications, Inc., 1997.

Gach, Michael Reed. *Acupressure for Lovers: Secrets of Touch for Increasing Intimacy*. New York: Bantam Books, 1997.

Gannon, Sharon, and David Life. *Jivamukti Yoga: Practices for Liberating Body and Soul*. New York: Ballantine Books, 2002.

Geshe, Kelsang Gyatso. *Guide to Dakini Land: The Highest Yoga Tantra Practice of Buddha Vajrayogini*. London: Tharpa Publications, 1996.

Goswami, Amit. *The Self-Aware Universe: How Consciousness Creates the Material World*. New York: Jeremy P. Tarcher, 1995.

Gross, David. "A World of Strings." Hypermind. http://195.200.108.47/universe/content/gsst.htm.

Gunaratana, Bhante Henepola. *Eight Mindful Steps to Happiness: Walking the Buddha's Path*. Somerville, MA: Wisdom Publications, 2001.

———. *Mindfulness in Plain English*. Somerville, MA: Wisdom Publications, 2002.

Hagen, Steve. *Buddhism Plain and Simple*. New York: Broadway, 1998.

Hanh, Thich Nhat. *Heart of Buddha's Teaching*. New York: Broadway, 1999.

Heartbeat 2000. "Heart of the Matter." Heartbeat 2000. http://www.heartbeat2000.com/hi.htm.

Henderson, Julie. *The Lover Within: Opening to Energy in Sexual Practice*. Barrytown, NY: Barrytown Limited, 1999.

Herrigel, Eugen. *Zen in the Art of Archery*. New York: Vintage, 1999.

Hittleman, Richard. *Richard Hittleman's Yoga: 28 Day Exercise Plan*. New York: Workman Publishing Company, 1972.

Intellimed International Corporation. "Human Anatomy Online." http://www.innerbody.com/htm/body.html.

Isherwood, Christopher. *Vedanta for the Western World*. Hollywood, CA: Vedanta Press, 1985.

Isherwood, Christopher, and Swami Prabhavananda, trans. *Bhagavad-Gita: The Song of God*. New York: Signet Classics, 2002.

———. *How to Know God: The Yoga Aphorisms of Patanjali*. Hollywood, CA: Vedanta Press, 1996.

Iyengar, B. K. S., and Yehudi Menuhin. *Light on Yoga: The Bible of Modern Yoga*. New York: Schocken, 1995.

Levine, Stephen. *Healing into Life and Death*. New York: Anchor Books, 1989.

———. *Meetings at the Edge: Dialogues with the Grieving and the Dying, the Healing and the Healed*. New York: Anchor Books, 1989.

———. *A Year to Live: How to Live This Year as If It Were Your Last*. New York: Harmony/Bell Tower, 1998.

Levine, Stephen, and Ondrea Levine. *Who Dies? An Investigation of Conscious Living and Conscious Dying*. New York: Anchor Books, 1989.

Lewis, Dennis. *Free Your Breath, Free Your Life: How Conscious Breathing Can Relieve Stress, Increase Vitality, and Help You Live More Fully*. Boston: Shambhala, 2004.

———. *The Tao of Natural Breathing: For Health, Well-Being and Inner Growth*. San Francisco: Mountain Wind Publishing, 1996.

Lilly, John C. *Center of the Cyclone*. New York: Random House, 1985.

———. *Programming the Human Biocomputer*. Berkeley, CA: Ronin Publishing, 2004.

McAfee, John. *The Secret of the Yamas: A Spiritual Guide to Yoga*. Woodland Park, CO: McAfee Publications, 2001.

McCracken, Thomas, ed. *New Atlas of Human Anatomy*. New York: Barnes & Noble Books, 1999.

Merrell-Wolff, Franklin. *Pathways through to Space*. New York: Three Rivers Press, 1983.

———. *The Philosophy of Consciousness Without an Object: Reflections on the Nature of Transcendental Consciousness*. New York: Julian Press, 1973.

Morgan, Marlo. *Mutant Message Down Under*. New York: HarperPerennial, 1994.

National Association of Anorexia Nervosa and Associated Disorders (ANAD). "Facts about Eating Disorders." Eating Disorder Info & Resources: General Information (2004). http://www.anad.org /site/anadweb/ content.php?type=1&id=6982#facts.

Odier, Daniel. *Nirvana Tao: The Secret Meditation Techniques of the Taoist and Buddhist Masters*. Rochester, VT: Inner Traditions, 1986.

———. "Shakti's Presence as Flames in the Heart." Letter to Tantrikas (December 2003). http://www.danielodier.com/ tantrikas_e3.htm (site now discontinued).

Odier, Daniel, and Clare Marie Frock, trans. *Desire: The Tantric Path to Awakening*. Rochester, VT: Inner Traditions, 2001.

———. *Yoga Spandakarika: The Sacred Texts at the Origins of Tantra*. Rochester, VT: Inner Traditions, 2005.

Odier, Daniel, and Jody Gladding, trans. *Tantric Quest: An Encounter with Absolute Love*. Rochester, VT: Inner Traditions, 1997.

Oliver, Mary. "Wild Geese." *Dream Work*. New York: Atlantic Monthly Press, 1986.

Ornish, Dean. *Love and Survival: The Scientific Basis for the Healing Power of Intimacy*. New York: HarperCollins, 1998.

Osho. *From Sex to Superconsciousness*. New Delhi: Osho World, 1979. http://www.oshoworld .com/e-books/ebooks.asp.

Pert, Candace B. *Molecules of Emotion: The Science Behind Mind-Body Medicine*. New York: Touchstone/Simon and Schuster, 1997.

Pirsig, Robert M. *Zen and the Art of Motorcycle Maintenance: An Inquiry into Values*. New York: Perennial, 2000.

Poole, Lawrence. "A Bit of a Giggle." *The Jungle Times* 1, no. 2 (March 2001). http://www .consult-IIDC.com/english/whatlinks/ newsletter2.htm.

Prescott, James W. "Anti-Social, Aggressive and Violence-Related Behaviors and Their Consequences." Presentation to research panel at the Center for Science Policy Studies, National Institutes of Health, Bethesda, Maryland (September 1993). http://www.birthpsychology.com/violence/prescott.html.

———. "Body Pleasure and the Origins of Violence." *The Futurist* (April 1975). Also appears in *The Bulletin of the Atomic Scientists* (November 1975).

———. "The Origins of Human Love and Violence." *Pre- and Perinatal Psychology Journal* (Institute of Humanistic Science) 10, no. 3 (Spring 1996).

Puthoff, H. E. "CIA-Initiated Remote Viewing at Stanford Research Institute." Superpowers of the Human Biomind. http://www.biomindsuperpowers.com/Pages/CIA-InitiatedRV.html.

Rajneesh, Bhagwan Shree. *Tantra, the Supreme Understanding: Discourses on the Tantric Way of Tilopa's Song of Mahamudra.* Rajneeshpuram, OR: Rajneesh Foundation International, 1984.

Reps, Paul. *Zen Flesh, Zen Bones.* Boston: Shambhala, 1994.

Richardson, Diana. *Tantric Orgasm for Women.* Rochester, VT: Park Street Press, 2004.

Roshi, Philip Kapleau. *The Three Pillars of Zen: Teaching, Practice, and Enlightenment.* New York: Anchor Books, 1989.

Salzberg, Sharon. *Lovingkindness: The Revolutionary Art of Happiness.* Boston: Shambhala, 1997.

Saraswati, Swami Satyananda. *Kundalini Tantra.* Munger, Bihar, India: Yoga Publications Trust, 2001.

———. *Meditations from the Tantras.* Munger, Bihar, India: Yoga Publications Trust, 2001.

Sarita, Ma Ananda, and Swami Anand Geho. *Ecstatic Sex: A Guide to the Pleasures of Tantra.* New York: Fireside, 2003.

———. *Tantric Love: A Nine-Step Guide to Transforming Lovers into Soul Mates.* New York: Fireside, 2001.

Schiffmann, Erich. *Yoga: The Spirit and Practice of Moving into Stillness.* New York: Pocket, 1996.

Spitz, René. *The First Year of Life.* New York: International University Press, 1965.

Starhawk. *The Spiral Dance.* New York: Harper-Collins, 1999.

Suryananda, D. Yogini Padma Ushas. "A Few Thoughts Regarding the Tantric Path." Sexuality.org: Society for Human Sexuality. http://www.sexuality.org/l/tantra/path.html.

Suzuki, D. T. *An Introduction to Zen Buddhism.* New York: Grove/Atlantic, 1991.

Tigunait, Pandit Rajmani. *Sakti: The Power in Tantra; A Scholarly Approach.* Honesdale, PA: Himalayan Institute Press, 1998.

Tirumular. "Tantra Seven." In *Tirumantiram,* translated by B. Natarajan. Kauai, HI: Himalaya Academy, n.d. http://www.himalayanacademy.com/resources/books/tirumantiram/TantraSeven.html.

Tripurari, Swami B. V. *Aesthetic Vedanta: The Sacred Path of Passionate Love.* San Rafael, CA: Mandala Publishing, 1998.

Watson, Burton, trans. *The Zen Teachings of Master Lin-Chi.* New York: Columbia University Press, 1999.

Watson, Cynthia Mervis. *Love Potions: A Guide to Aphrodisiacs and Sexual Pleasures.* New York: Jeremy P. Tarcher, 1993.

Watts, Alan. *Behold the Spirit: A Study in the Necessity of Mystical Religion*. New York: Vintage, 1972.

————. *Buddhism: The Religion of No-Religion; The Edited Transcripts*. North Clarendon, VT: Tuttle Publishing, 1999.

————. *Cloud-Hidden: Whereabouts Unknown; A Mountain Journal*. New York: Vintage, 1974.

————. *Nature, Man and Woman*. New York: Vintage, 1991.

————. *Psychotherapy East and West*. New York: Vintage, 1975.

————. *This Is It, and Other Essays on Zen and Spiritual Experience*. New York: Vintage, 1973.

————. *The Way of Zen*. New York: Vintage, 1999.

————. *The Wisdom of Insecurity*. New York: Vintage, 1968.

Watts, Alan, and Al Chung-Liang Huang. *Tao: The Watercourse Way*. New York: Pantheon, 1977.

Wei, Wei Wu. *Why Lazarus Laughed: The Essential Doctrine; Zen–Advaita–Tantra*. Boulder, CO: Sentient Publications, 2004.

White, David Gordon, ed. *Tantra in Practice*. Princeton, NJ: Princeton University Press, 2000.

Wong, Eva. *The Shambhala Guide to Taoism*. Boston: Shambhala, 1996.

Yeshe, Lama. *Introduction to Tantra: The Transformation of Desire*. Edited by Jonathan Landaw. Foreword by Philip Glass. Somerville, MA: Wisdom Publications, 2001.

About the Authors

Al Link and Pala Copeland have been leading retreats on sacred loving for ten years. As experts on the subject of sexuality and Tantra, they have appeared on radio and television and have contributed to many publications, such as *Ladies' Home Journal, Redbook, Body and Soul,* and the *Wall Street Journal.* They live in Ottawa, Canada. Visit their website at www.tantra-sex.com.

To Write to the Authors

If you wish to contact the authors or would like more information about this book, please write to the authors in care of Llewellyn Worldwide and we will forward your request. Both the authors and publisher appreciate hearing from you and learning of your enjoyment of this book and how it has helped you. Llewellyn Worldwide cannot guarantee that every letter written to the authors can be answered, but all will be forwarded. Please write to:

Al Link & Pala Copeland
℅ Llewellyn Worldwide
2143 Wooddale Drive, Dept. 0-7387-0965-4
Woodbury, MN 55125-2989, U.S.A.

Please enclose a self-addressed stamped envelope for reply,
or $1.00 to cover costs. If outside U.S.A., enclose
international postal reply coupon.

Many of Llewellyn's authors have websites with additional information and resources. For more information, please visit our website at:

www.llewellyn.com